CHRIS RYAN

CHRIS RYAN
SAS HERO

- **Joined the SAS in 1984, serving in military hot zones across the world.**

- **Expert in overt and covert operations in war zones, including Northern Ireland, Africa, the Middle East and other classified territories.**

- **Commander of the Sniper squad within the anti-terrorist team.**

- **Part of an 8-man patrol on the Bravo Two Zero Gulf War mission in Iraq.**

- **The mission was compromised. 3 fellow soldiers died, and 4 more were captured as POWs. Ryan was the only person to defy the enemy, evading capture and escaping to Syria on foot over a distance of 300 kilometres.**

- **His ordeal made history as the longest escape and evasion by an SAS trooper, for which he was awarded the Military Medal.**

- **His books are dedicated to the men and women who risk their lives fighting for the armed forces.**

THE ONE THAT GOT AWAY

CHRIS RYAN

SAS HERO

RED FOX

*Also available by Chris Ryan, and published by
Random House Children's Books:*

CODE RED
Flash Flood
Wildfire
Outbreak
Vortex
Twister
Battleground

ALPHA FORCE
Survival
Rat-Catcher
Desert Pursuit
Hostage
Red Centre
Hunted
Blood Money
Fault Line
Black Gold
Untouchable

Published by the Random House Group for adult readers:

NON-FICTION
The One That Got Away
Chris Ryan's SAS Fitness Book
Chris Ryan's Ultimate Survival Guide
Fight to Win: Deadly Skills of the Elite Forces

FICTION
Stand By, Stand By
Zero Option
The Kremlin Device
Tenth Man Down
Hit List
The Watchman
Land of Fire
Greed
The Increment
Blackout
Ultimate Weapon
Strike Back
Firefight
Who Dares Wins
One Good Turn *(Adult Quick Read for World Book Day 2008)*

For Sarah

THE ONE THAT GOT AWAY
A RED FOX BOOK 978 1 849 41346 6

First published in Great Britain by Red Fox,
an imprint of Random House Children's Books
A Random House Group Company
This edition published 2010

1 3 5 7 9 10 8 6 4 2

Adapted for younger readers from *The One That Got Away*,
first published in the UK in 1995 by Century, an imprint of Cornerstone,
a Random House Group Company.

The Random House Group Limited supports the Forest Stewardship Council (FSC),
the leading international forest certification organization. All our titles that are
printed on Greenpeace-approved FSC-certified paper carry the FSC logo.
Our paper procurement policy can be found at www.rbooks.co.uk/environment.

Mixed Sources
Product group from well-managed
forests and other controlled sources
www.fsc.org Cert no. TT-COC-2139
© 1996 Forest Stewardship Council

Set in Adobe Garamond 13.5 / 17.5 pt

Red Fox Books are published by Random House Children's Books,
61–63 Uxbridge Road, London W5 5SA

www.**kids**at**randomhouse**.co.uk
www.**rbooks**.co.uk

Addresses for companies within The Random House Group Limited can be found at:
www.randomhouse.co.uk/offices.htm

THE RANDOM HOUSE GROUP Limited Reg. No. 954009

A CIP catalogue record for this book is available from the British Library.

Printed and bound in Great Britain by CPI Bookmarque, Croydon, CR0 4TD

THE ONE THAT GOT AWAY

GLOSSARY

Bergen	*Haversack*
Bivvy bag	*A cross between a sleeping bag and a tent*
Casevac	*Casualty evacuation*
CO	*Commanding officer of the regiment*
Comms	*Communications*
Contact	*In action against the enemy, using weapons*
Director, the	*Officer commanding Special Forces, generally a brigadier*
Dishdash	*Cotton robes, worn by people in the Middle East who live or work in deserts*
DPM	*Disruptive pattern material camouflage clothes*
Escape map	*A lightweight map with basic details, carried on operations*
FMB	*Forward Mounting Base*
GPS	*Global positioning system*
Gulf War	*A war between Iraq (led by Saddam Hussein) and 34 coalition countries who were against the Iraqi invasion of Kuwait. It lasted 2 August 1990–28 February 1991*
Int	*Intelligence*
Laager point	*A camp, especially one surrounded by a ring of vehicles*
Loadie	*Crewman on RAF military flight*
LUP	*Lying-up point*
Mag	*Weapons magazine, holding rounds*
NBC	*Nuclear, biological and chemical*
OC	*Officer commanding the squadron*
OP	*Observation post*
Regiment, the	*The SAS*
Rounds	*Bullets*
RV	*Rendezvous*
Sangar	*Fortified enclosure*
Satcom	*Telephone using satellite transmission*
Scuds	*Missiles, transported and fired from mobile launchers*
Shamag	*Shawl used by Arabs as a headdress*
SOP	*Standard operating procedure*
SP Team	*Special projects or counter-terrorist team*
SQMS	*Squadron Quartermaster Sergeant*

SSM	*Squadron Sergeant Major*
Stand By	*To get ready for action*
Stag	*Sentry duty*
Tabbing	*Progressing at speed across country, often with heavy loads*
TACBE	*Tactical rescue beacon*
TEL	*Transporter-erector-launcher vehicle*
Wadi	*A watercourse in a desert region; dry, except in the rainy season*
Zero a weapon	*To set your sights to ensure the weapon is accurate*

MILITARY HARDWARE

Tristar	*Aircraft used for air transport and in-air refuelling*
Hercules	*Large plane, used for troop transports*
Chinook	*Helicopter with two rotary blades*
B-52	*US bomber plane*

WEAPONS

203	*Combination of 5.56 calibre automatic rifle (top barrel) and 40 mm grenade launcher below*
.50	*Heavy machine gun*
66	*Disposable rocket launcher*
AK-47	*Assault rifle, first developed in the Soviet Union by Kalashnikov*
Claymore mines	*Anti-personnel mines; unlike more conventional landmines, the claymore fires metal balls like a shotgun*
GPMG	*General-purpose machine gun, also known as a 'gympi'*
LAW 90	*Rocket launcher*
Minimi	*5.56 calibre machine gun*
M19	*Rapid-fire grenade launcher*
SA80	*British small arms (Small Arms for the 80s); includes rifles that are the standard issue for the British Army*

CONTENTS

'You have personally made SAS history.'

General Peter de la Billière,
Director of UK Special Forces,
Commander in Chief British Forces

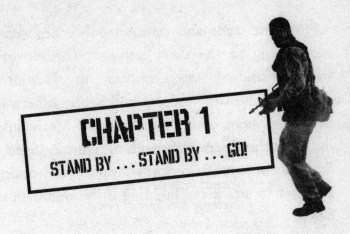

CHAPTER 1
STAND BY ... STAND BY ... GO!

Our target was a disused mental hospital.

Five terrorists were inside, holding nine hostages captive. After a three-day siege, matters were moving swiftly to a head.

As commander of the SAS eight-man sniper team of 'B' Squadron, I was in charge of seven other men. We were positioned with our rifles at observation points in outhouses, trees and on the ground. Two men were watching each face of the hospital and sending back running commentaries over their throat-mike radios to the command centre. This had been set up in a separate building 200 metres from the front door. Each face of the hospital had been given a special code so that everyone knew which bit they were talking about.

From the command centre a police negotiator was talking to the chief terrorist. The terrorist was demanding safe conduct to Heathrow airport for himself and his colleagues; otherwise he would shoot one of the hostages. Meanwhile, the military officer commanding the SP (Special Projects, or counter-terrorist) team was working out how to attack the building if the negotiations failed.

Suddenly a shot cracked out from within the hospital. A hostage had been executed. The terrorists called for a stretcher party to take the body away. The front door opened briefly, and a limp figure was bundled out. A four-man team ran over to collect it. Then the chief terrorist threatened to kill another hostage in half an hour if his demands were not met.

The moment had come for the police to hand over to the military. The police chief signed a written order passing command to the OC (Officer Commanding) of 'B' Squadron, the senior SAS officer present. The OC then gave the three eight-man assault teams their orders. The moment he had finished, the men moved to their entry points.

Now it was just a question of waiting for my snipers to get as many terrorists in their sights as possible. Listening to our commentaries on the radio, the OC suddenly called out the order we'd all been waiting for:

'I have control. STAND BY . . . STAND BY . . . GO!'

For the past two days the grounds of the old hospital had been eerily silent. Now the whole place erupted into action. Two vehicles screamed up to the building and a swarm of black-clad assaulters jumped out. Explosive charges blew in the windows. Within seconds, a Chinook helicopter was poised above the roof and more black figures were fast-roping out of it, abseiling down to the windows or entering through the skylights. Stun grenades blasted off; smoke poured out. The radio carried a babble of shots, shouts, explosions and orders.

In a matter of minutes the building had been cleared, the five terrorists killed and the remaining eight hostages rescued. The assault commander reported that he had control, and command was formally handed back to the police.

* * *

On this occasion, this had all been just an exercise – but as always, the assault had been realistic in every detail, and had been excellent training. Just another day for the Regiment, as members of the SAS refer to themselves. And exactly the kind of task we could at any time be called upon to perform, efficiently and explosively. Practice was essential.

'Well done, everybody,' the OC told us. 'That was pretty good.'

We packed our kit into the vehicles and set out for SAS headquarters in Hereford. But on the way events took an unexpected turn.

It was 2 August 1990, and on the news we heard that Saddam Hussein, the tyrannical leader of Iraq, had just invaded Kuwait, a small country on his southern border.

'So what?' said one of the guys scornfully. 'Saddam's an idiot.'

'Don't be too sure of it,' said someone else. 'It'll make big trouble, and we'll probably find ourselves out there.'

He was right. Saddam's invasion of Kuwait was the opening salvo of the 1990–1991 Gulf War. I don't think any of us realized just how this news would change our lives.

* * *

For the next two months, nobody knew what was going to happen. The leaders of different governments around the world got together to discuss the situation and the UN Security Council called for Iraq to withdraw from Kuwait – and gave them a deadline. When the Iraqis did not leave Kuwait, a war was inevitable. In total thirty-four countries joined together in a coalition to oppose Saddam Hussein. These countries included not only the USA and Great Britain but also Arab countries in the Middle East region, like Egypt and Syria.

'A' and 'D' Squadron went out to the Gulf for build-up training; but me and my mates in 'B' Squadron were told we wouldn't be going, as it was our turn to take over what are known in the SAS as team tasks – assignments for which small teams of men are needed in various parts of the world.

The SAS is made up of four squadrons – A, B, D and G. Each squadron is made up of four troops – Air Troop, Mountain Troop, Boat Troop and Mobility Troop. There should be sixteen men in each troop, but because it is so difficult to get into the SAS, there are often as few as eight.

Rumours started to fly. Some people said we might become sky-marshals on civilian flights to the Middle East. It would mean pretending to be normal passengers, but in fact carrying weapons to deal with any terrorist who might attempt a hijack. The idea seemed quite likely – on the SP team we'd done lots of assaults on and inside aircraft, so we knew what to do.

But then, a week before Christmas, we were dragged into the briefing room at Hereford and told that half of 'B' Squadron was going to deploy to the Middle East after all.

That meant me.

When I heard the news, I went home and said to Janet, my wife: 'Listen, we're heading out.' Normally, as so many missions are top secret, SAS guys say nothing to their wives and families about what they're doing, but in this case it was obvious where we were going. After Saddam's invasion of Kuwait, there had been so much coverage on television and in the newspapers, our destination could only have been the Gulf.

Christmas was not a relaxed time. The Regiment was stood-to throughout the holiday period, and we were busy getting our 'green' kit ready. In the

SAS, 'green' refers to normal military operations, as opposed to 'black' work, like that on the SP team, for which you wear black gear from head to foot. I'd been in black roles for at least three years, so now I brought my webbing and bergen home to paint them in desert camouflage colours. We were having an extension built onto our house, and a builder called John was digging the footings. Seeing me at work outside, he came up and asked what I was doing.

'Just painting my webbing.'

'Those colours are a bit light, aren't they?'

'Well,' I said carefully, 'you'd be surprised. It works quite well.' In fact, he was right: I had the colours too light and sandy, as I was to find out to my cost.

Packing our kit took some time. All our weapons were bundled together and went separately, rolled up in canvas sleeves. When I asked the squadron quartermaster (SQMS) if he'd included pistols, he said, 'Yeah, twenty of them.' I was glad about that, because pistols were essential back-up weapons. We would need them if our own weapons failed or if we were caught in a confined space like a vehicle, or an observation post. Most of us would be carrying either M16 203s – a combination of a 5.56 calibre automatic rifle in the top barrel and a grenade launcher below – or Minimi machine guns. Both are over a metre long and awkward to handle or conceal.

As I was sorting my personal equipment, I asked the SQMS if I could take some cold-weather mountaineering gear.

'Nah,' he replied. 'You're going to the desert! It won't be cold there.' Little did he know what the winter in Iraq would be like. I kept thinking that we might end up at high altitudes, in the mountains of northern Iraq on the Turkish border, where snow might be lying. It was as if I had some premonition. But I did nothing about it, and most of us didn't take any cold-weather gear at all.

At last we heard that we were to fly out.

On the night of Saturday 5 January 1991, a Tristar took us from RAF Brize Norton, landed at Cyprus to refuel, then flew on to the Gulf, where it taxied up behind a hangar. Getting off into the warm night, we found the OC, the Squadron Sergeant Major (SSM) and the SQMS lined up waiting for us at the bottom of the steps, all wearing desert kit or Arab shawls called shamags, wrapped round their necks like scarves. It was our first sight of anyone dressed like that, and it brought home to us where we were.

A Hercules was parked alongside and we jumped into the back. There were no seats or straps, so we sat on the metal deck for the short flight up to our Forward Mounting Base (FMB), known as Victor. This was near Abu Dhabi in the United Arab Emirates.

'Hold tight,' said the loadie. 'We're going to do an operational take-off.'

The pilot revved his engines until they were screaming and the whole aircraft began to judder; then he let go his brakes and we were hurled forward and heaved into the air. Fifteen minutes later he went diving in and landed with a couple of heavy thumps, slowing down violently.

At FMB Victor, a hangar became our temporary home. There was a heap of bergens, weapons piled in big rolls, a stack of American cots, boxes of radios, medical kit and demolition equipment. Everything looked as though it had arrived just that minute.

The OC told us it wasn't clear how we were

going to be deployed. 'A' and 'D' Squadrons were already well advanced with their build-up training for deployment behind Iraqi lines. They were out in the desert preparing their weapons, including .50 Browning heavy machine guns, mortars, LAW 90 rocket launchers, Milan anti-tank missile launchers and – most effective of all – M19s, which are high-speed grenade launchers, in effect machine guns firing bombs.

As for 'B' Squadron, the OC said he hoped to get us a few vehicles, which we would have to convert for desert operations. He promised to keep us updated on the way things were looking, then told us to get our heads down before we started training next day. We each found a cot and set it up against the wall of the hangar, with mosquito nets rigged on poles above. That was to be our home for the next ten days.

Morning revealed that we were well out in the desert, at one of several different camps dotted about a vast training area. Most of the desert was a flat plain of hard, beige-coloured sand, but every now and then runs of low dunes broke the monotony; on these ridges, which were maybe ten metres high, a few tufts of dry grass and the odd tree were growing, and the sand was very soft, so that vehicles often got stuck.

Approaching Victor from the desert, you came over a rise. There was a high chain-link fence surrounding large hangars and a runway, with sand dunes lapping the perimeter wire. At night the perimeter was brightly illuminated. The base had originally been built as a parachute school. The hangars were for storage of chutes and other equipment, and there were tall towers for hanging chutes out to dry.

We began build-up training, and there was plenty to organize: radios, satellite communications and NBC (nuclear, biological and chemical warfare) drills. As a trained medic, I set up some medical instruction: teaching guys how to put drips in, how to pack gunshot wounds to stop bleeding, how to treat heat exhaustion. To demonstrate intravenous techniques, I grabbed a 'volunteer' from the front row, choosing someone lean, because he had prominent veins. The SAS might be tough, but it's not unknown for someone to faint when it comes to injections!

We were given jabs against anthrax – a deadly

biological warfare agent. The vaccine made everyone feel terrible for three or four days, with bad bruising in the arm that had been injected. One man's arm remained black and blue for six weeks, and some people had muscle around the puncture actually go rotten three or four weeks after the jab. Several guys had to be dragged back out of the field for minor surgery. I was lucky, and got nothing worse than a cold and a burning throat; but I kept waking up in the night, coughing up lumps of phlegm the size of golf balls.

Most of our training took place inside our hangar, but we also went on the firing ranges to zero our weapons, which included 203s, Minimi machine guns and the more powerful general-purpose machine guns (GPMGs, known as gympis), which fire 7.62 rounds. Gympis have a greater range and are harder-hitting than the Minimis. There was one set of ranges only a couple of hundred metres away, and a larger complex three hours out into the desert. We'd fired the weapons already on a gallery range in Hereford, but because they'd all been packed up, loaded and unloaded several times, we needed to zero them again.

We were out in the Gulf, training hard and preparing our weapons. But none of us knew what the future held for us.

It didn't take long for all that to change.

CHAPTER 2
BRAVO TWO ZERO!

On the night of the 16–17 January, after the United Nations deadline of 15 January had passed and Saddam Hussein had not withdrawn his troops from Kuwait – coalition aircraft started bombing targets in Iraq. The air war had begun.

Almost immediately, Saddam Hussein started firing Scud missiles into Israel. He had to be stopped.

Saddam's Scuds were being launched from mobile missile launchers, but neither satellites nor aircraft could find them. Suddenly the Regiment had a vital role to perform: to find the mobile launchers and stop the bombardment of Israel.

The big Special Forces punch was to come from 'A' and 'D' Squadrons. They would go in as substantial motorized patrols, each heavily armed and half a squadron strong. Their job would be to find the Scud TELs (transporter-erector-launchers), then call in Allied aircraft to blow them up. But first, three eight-man patrols from 'B' Squadron, designated Bravo One Zero, Bravo Two Zero and Bravo Three Zero, would infiltrate deep into Iraqi territory. They would lie up in OPs (observation posts) to report enemy movement, especially that of Scuds.

I was to be part of the Bravo Two Zero patrol. We were selected according to our particular skills: besides fighting power, we needed a demolitionist, a signaller and a medic (myself). The main task would be to gather intelligence. Our aim was to find a good lying-up position (LUP) and set up an OP to maintain surveillance on the main supply route, which ran westwards from the town of Al Hadithah to three airfields known as H1, H2 and H3, and along which it was thought the Iraqis were moving Scud launchers. Each patrol's plan, in fact, was to put in two OPs, one covering the other, fifty or a hundred metres apart and linked by telephone line. One would have an observation opening facing forward onto the main supply route. The other would be in front of it with the opening facing backwards. That way, the guys there could watch the ground behind their colleagues.

We would remain in the OP for up to ten days, reporting enemy movements by radio or Satcom telephone, and calling in fighter-bombers to attack any worthwhile target. We were also told to blow up any fibre-optic communications links we could find. After ten days, we would either get a re-supply by helicopter, or move to a new location, also by chopper.

Besides all our personal equipment, we would take kit for building the OP: 120 empty sandbags per man, vehicle camouflage nets, poles, and thermal sheets to put over the top of our structures, so that if Iraqis flew over with thermal-imaging devices they wouldn't be able to pick up the heat rising from our bodies.

As we were preparing ourselves, it became clear that the Regiment didn't have enough equipment to go around. I told the SQMS that we needed some 203 rounds to fire from the grenade-launching part of our weapons.

'Well,' he replied, 'we haven't got any.'

'Why not?'

'There are just none here.'

In fact, there were plenty of 203 rounds, but other people had them. I had to borrow twelve from a mate of mine in 'A' Squadron.

It was the same with claymore mines, which we wanted as a deterrent to put the brakes on anyone trying to come after us in the desert. (If you're being followed, you can put down a mine with a timer, and crack it off after maybe five minutes. Even if it doesn't do any damage, it slows people down, because they wonder if there are more mines in front of them.) When we asked for claymores, the answer was that there weren't any, and someone told us to make our own out of ammunition boxes packed with plastic explosives and gympi link – the metal belt that holds machine-gun rounds together.

This was ridiculous: home-made devices like that are crude, large and heavy, and we had no room to carry them. Later, however, we did make a single claymore out of plastic ice-cream cartons, and one of us took it in his bergen.

In the end we were given a mixed load of stuff by the Special Boat Service: five claymores, a box of

L2 grenades, a box of white phosphorus grenades and some 66 rockets. We shared out some of this with the other two patrols, and I myself finished up with one L2 grenade and two white phosphorus.

We were also missing pistols. The twenty pistols packed and shipped for our own use simply disappeared, nicked for the other squadrons. The result was that the only man in our unit with a pistol was a guy called Vince, who had brought it with him from 'A' Squadron. We also asked for silenced pistols, and in particular for the make invented during the Second World War for Special Operations Executives. Although fairly basic, these have never been surpassed for sheer quietness – no more than a *pfft* – and at close range the 9 mm slug is deadly. The other two squadrons had such weapons and, as things turned out, there were several moments when I could have done with one.

We were also missing other basic equipment. Take the maps, for instance. The only maps we had were really poor and designed for air crews. Their scale (1:250,000) was so small that they showed few details. They might have helped navigators, but they were no good to people on the ground. To back them up, we badly needed satellite information, but we were told that no satellite imagery was available.

The first escape maps we were given had been printed in 1928, then updated for the Second World War. At the last minute, though, we were issued with newer ones, printed on silk, which we worked into the waistbands of our trousers.

Each of us was given a photocopied note, in Arabic and English, promising £5,000 to anyone who handed over a Coalition serviceman to a friendly power. Deciding the document was rubbish, I threw mine away. Later, however, I changed my mind; because I couldn't speak Arabic, I thought I'd better have a note after all. So I got another member of the patrol, Bob Consiglio, to photocopy his, and I took that with me. We also signed for twenty gold sovereigns each, in case we had to bribe somebody or buy our way out of trouble. Of course, we were supposed to return these after the conflict, but not everybody did.

The patrol's main task would be to man the OP, but we knew we might also have to blow up fibre-optic communication lines. Luckily one of our lads knew about fibre-optic cables. He told us that we needed a particular device, like a metal detector, for tracing them. We asked for one immediately. He also knew that if a cable is cut, the operators can tell where the break is. We therefore decided that, if we did blow a line, we would put anti-personnel mines around the break, so that when engineers came to repair it they would be taken out. We would also lay another delayed-action device to blow the line again later. But the main aim of the exercise would be to kill as many skilled personnel as possible. If we managed to kill the first wave coming out to make repairs, it was a good bet that the next lot would say they couldn't find the break, and the line would remain cut.

Bravo Two Zero was to be commanded by Sergeant Andy McNab. Andy was then about thirty-two, a Cockney Jack-the-Lad with such a gift of the gab that he could talk his way out of any situation. Dark-haired, with a moustache, he'd done a lot of work in the Regiment and was a good demolitionist.

Paired off with Andy – which meant he shared bed-spaces, vehicles, cooking equipment and so on – was Dinger, a lance corporal of twenty-eight who'd been in the Parachute Regiment. A bit of a wild character, he was always game for a fight. If you described anyone as mad, or as a joker, it would be him. Yet he was also a good family man, married with two daughters.

The other sergeant was Vince, an older man, about thirty-five, a medic like myself, who tended to be a bit nervous and twitchy in his movements. He was tall and slim, with an athletic build; he had fuzzy, dark-gingery hair and a drooping, Mexican-type moustache. He came from Swindon, and was married with three children. He was putting a bold front on things, but I knew his heart wasn't in this operation. Only a few days before, we'd sat on his camp-bed and he'd said to me, 'I don't want to be doing this.'

We discussed things a bit, and I said to him, 'Well, now that we're here, we'd better just get on with it and hope we'll come out OK at the end.' I got the impression that he wanted to finish his time in the army and be done with the whole business.

A closer friend of mine was Trooper Bob Consiglio. Twenty-four years old, the son of a Sicilian father and an English mother, he was very small (only 5 foot 5 inches – or 1.65 metres) but incredibly strong, with a heart like a lion. He was a really nice lad, and would do anything you told him to. He was a hard worker and a cheerful character. When it came to fighting, Bob wasn't frightened of anything. I said to him one day, 'Bob, if anything happens when we're in there, make sure you stick with me.' It wasn't that I didn't trust him to do anything by himself, though I did want to protect him, almost as if he were a brother. Rather, because he was so brave, it would be to my own advantage to have him close.

Twice Bob's size was Stan – a different character entirely. He was over six foot tall (1.8 metres plus), not that obviously muscular, but very, very strong, well-spoken and a gentleman. Nothing ever seemed to bother him; whatever happened, his voice kept the same tone, and he just got on with things. If he had a fault, it was that he was too nice. He was another good mate of mine, and I wouldn't have liked to see him get angry, because he could be a formidable fighter.

The other two members of the patrol were Legs Lane – so called because he was tall and thin – and Mark, a keen New Zealander who had joined the squadron only a month before. Both were very quiet, but they were good men, and Mark especially was always game for anything. Legs was a key man in the patrol as he was carrying the 319, the main radio set.

Finally there was myself: a Geordie from near Newcastle, aged twenty-eight, and a corporal. During six years in the regular SAS I'd gained a good deal of useful experience in many countries, and at the beginning of 1991 I was physically the strongest I'd ever been, because during my last tour with the SP team I'd hit the weights and built up a lot of muscle on my upper body. The extra strength had been useful, because in the SP team you're forever going up ropes or sliding down them, climbing into buildings, carrying guys, jumping off vehicles, pushing people away or restraining them. In all this, you're handling a lot of weight. In your black kit, you have your body armour, Kevlar helmet, and waistcoat loaded with ammunition, stun grenades and axes, besides your machine gun and pistol. My weight had gone up from 11 to 12½ stone – that's from about 70 kilos to nearly 80 kilos. Little did I know that the extra muscle was going to save my life.

In our last days at Victor we were busier than ever. Andy was getting the demolition kit sorted. I saw to the medical packs, Legs Lane to the radio. Everyone scrounged ammunition. We were told that when we moved up to Al Jouf – a Regiment Forward Operating Base (FOB), in an airfield in the north-west of Saudi Arabia – we would go more or less straight over the border into Iraq. Everything had to be ready before we left. We were told to leave all our non-essential kit behind.

On the evening of 18 January we flew to Al Jouf in three Hercules transport planes. On board were all the squadron vehicles and stores. The air war was then at its height, raging for the third night, and there was quite a high risk of being shot at en route. The sky was full of armed warplanes, all trying to blow the opposition out of the air.

When we landed at Al Jouf, the first thing we noticed was the wind. It was much colder there. But because we'd been told we were going to deploy into Iraq immediately, we'd left most of our warm kit behind.

We began to unload our equipment and pile it in a grassed area that was like a garden, about thirty metres by twenty, next to one of the hangars. Someone told us we'd be sleeping that night in the grassy area; so we sorted out bivvy bags and sleeping bags, made a brew, and got our heads down in the open.

The night sky was clear, and as we lay there we watched streams of B-52s crossing high above us, with fighters skimming like minnows alongside. The sight sent my mind straight back to the time when, as a boy, I'd watched television pictures of B-52s going over in streams to bomb Vietnam. Now, as the aircraft reached the Iraqi border, their flashing lights were suddenly extinguished, but we heard the roar of massed jet engines rumble away into the distance. It was comforting to know that our aircraft were bombing the enemy. We hoped they would do enough damage to make Saddam capitulate before we were even deployed.

Morning showed that the airfield at Al Jouf was surrounded by security wire and primitive, flat-roofed wooden towers with glass windows, which reminded us of the German concentration camps we'd seen in Second World War films. There was one main terminal, quite small, with a few other buildings attached to it. Our regimental headquarters and all our stores were there, but we were billeted on the other side of the airfield. Here there was a cement building with a single washbasin and a hole in the ground to act as a toilet. It soon became blocked.

The SSM had been told to bring the squadron tents, but he had decided that, because we were in the desert and the weather would be hot, we wouldn't need them. Our first impressions had been correct, however: it wasn't hot at all; it was very cold, and the dust was everywhere. All we could do was sling cam nets from our vehicles for a bit of shelter, and we lived on the ground like pigs, huddled around the Land Rovers. We had no tables or chairs, so we ate our meals sitting on the deck, with the dust blowing around everywhere, covering us, our kit and our food.

We had no time for detailed planning but our task seemed fairly simple. Looking at our maps we could see that the site we'd chosen for our laying-up position was opposite a slight bend in the main supply route. It looked from the map as though we could dig into the bank of a wadi – a dried-up river bed – and have a view straight up the gully to the big road.

If we saw a Scud on the move, we were to report it immediately over the Satcom telephone, and follow up with a message on the 319 radio. Then aircraft would be launched or vectored to take the missile out. A brief on the missiles gave us an idea of what big beasts they were. Just over thirteen metres long and one metre in diameter, they would look a bit like fuel tankers when in the horizontal position on their trailers – the TELs. Apparently the Iraqis' habit was to park them alongside embankments or under road bridges so that they were all but invisible from the air. When on the move, a TEL would always be accompanied by other vehicles in a wide convoy.

Privately, we agreed that if we did find a convoy we would allow a few minutes to pass before we reported it – otherwise the Iraqis might work out where we were. And we were worried about what the Scud warheads might contain: if they were nuclear, or full of gas or biological agents, we didn't want to be around when they came apart. We were also nervous of using satellite communications, because a good direction-finding station can locate a transmitter within twenty seconds. We practised getting on the phone and reporting a Scud sighting in as few seconds as possible.

Bravo One Zero and Bravo Three Zero had decided to take vehicles in with them, but at the last minute we opted to go without. Over the past few days we had talked about it a lot. Obviously vehicles would enable us to drive out of trouble and back over the border if things went wrong, but nobody in the patrol thought that vehicles were essential. Looking back, though, I realize that I had a strong influence on the decision. I had made more OPs than all the rest of the guys in the patrol put together, and I considered myself something of an expert at the job. But I had never operated in the desert, and just couldn't see a small patrol like ours escaping detection if we were saddled with vehicles.

I realize now it was a big mistake to go without them. We should have driven in, installed an OP with a couple of men, then pulled off to a safe distance and hidden the vehicles under cam nets in the bottom of some deep wadi. That way, we would have been more mobile and could have loaded the vehicles up with powerful armaments, including heavy machine guns.

No vehicles also meant we had to carry huge individual loads. The average weight of a bergen was 60 kg. With that lot on, you had to walk with your head down like a donkey, so that you'd be useless in a contact, and if you fell over you'd be knackered.

But that wasn't all. Apart from the bergens, each of us had a belt-kit of pouches weighing 20 kg, and a whole load more gear that wouldn't fit in anywhere else: seven days' rations in one sandbag, two NBC suits in another, an extra bandolier of ammunition, extra grenades for the 203 launchers, and a jerry can of water. Altogether we had nearly 120 kg of kit each. To put that into context, that meant I was carrying about my full body weight plus half as much again!

Talking to the RAF helicopter pilots who were going to fly us in, we heard how they planned their routes into Iraq to avoid known anti-aircraft positions. With their help we identified the precise spot at which we wanted to be dropped. At first we chose a point five kilometres short of our lying-up position, but later, because of the weight of our kit, we changed our minds and asked to be put down only two or three kilometres short.

Arrangements for evacuation seemed straight-forward enough. If we had not come on the air within forty-eight hours of being dropped off, a chopper would come back to pick us up. If we needed casevac (casualty evacuation), a heli would come within twenty-four hours of any call. If we had a contact and needed assistance, half the squadron would be on board the helicopter to pull us out.

The OC tried to reassure us. 'Don't worry,' he said. 'You've got your three-one-nine radio. You've got your Satcom. You've got your tactical rescue beacons. 'A' and 'D' Squadrons are going to be in your area. Also, you've got the forty-eight-hour Lost Comms procedure, and the twenty-four-hour casevac.' That all sounded fine – but things didn't turn out quite as we hoped.

One detail to which we should have paid more attention was our cover story. We agreed that if we were captured, we would pretend to be members of a medical team, sent in to recover downed aircrew, or possibly members of a team sent to provide security for medics, and that our chopper had been forced down. The general idea was to stick as close to the truth as possible, but to say that we were reservists or ordinary infantrymen, and that we'd been brought into the war because we worked in a medical centre. Yet we never had time to work things out in any depth – to decide, for instance, which fictitious regiment we belonged to.

We went off in such a rush that when we boarded the Chinook on the evening of 19 January, Andy was still being briefed on the ramp at the back of the helicopter. (Bravo One Zero and Three Zero were to go in the next night.)

Guys from 'B' Squadron threw our kit into vehicles and came with us to the helicopter. I sensed a peculiar atmosphere. Nobody had much to say. As we were going on board, our mates were all around us, but I got the feeling that they thought this was a one-way ticket. Somebody said to me, 'This is ridiculous – it's not on, to carry loads like this.'

But by then it was too late to change things.

Off we went into the dusk, and after half an hour we landed at Arar, an airfield close to the Iraqi border, to refuel. When the pilot shut down his engines, we stayed where we were, in the back. Then came an incredible letdown. The engines started turning and burning again, we lifted off and were almost over the frontier when the pilot radioed for permission to cross.

It was denied.

He came on the intercom to announce, 'Sorry, guys. Mission aborted.' The Americans were bombing targets on our route, and we had to keep out of the way.

Having psyched ourselves up, we somehow had

to come down. Although everyone pretended to be disappointed, in fact the guys were relieved. We all looked at each other, and grins spread over our faces as we headed back to Al Jouf.

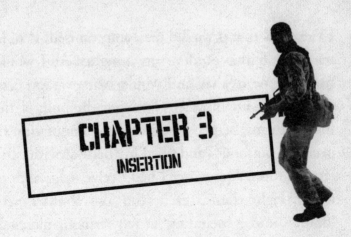

CHAPTER 3
INSERTION

As soon as we landed back, the guys started stripping their kit to try to save weight. Out went luxuries like sleeping bags and most of our warm clothes. We realized that the weather was much colder than at Victor, but our bergens were so heavy that the only way we could get them on was to sit down, settle the straps over our shoulders, and have a couple of the other guys pull us to our feet, as if they were lifting knights in armour onto their chargers.

I became obsessed with the need for ammunition. Pressured by the thought that we were going to be on our own behind enemy lines, I left food out of my belt-kit in favour of more rounds. Normally I carried twenty-four hours' worth of rations in a belt-pouch – enough to spread over four days – but

I reckoned that if we did get compromised, I could reach the Syrian border in two nights. All I would need on me in that case would be two packets of AB (army issue biscuits). So I put the bulk of the food into my bergen – resisting the temptation to overload on food – and filled my belt-kit with extra ammunition. Altogether I had twelve magazines of twenty-eight rounds each, and also about ninety loose rounds, including a few armour-piercing, which I'd brought from Hereford.

One of the items I threw out was my brew-kit: tea bags, sachets of coffee, orange powder, sugar and the fuel – inflammable hexi-blocks. We were going in on hard routine, which meant no cooking and no fires, so I thought I would have no chance to use anything like that. Another serious omission was puritabs, for sterilizing water. If we'd been going into the jungle, where you use local water all the time, I'd certainly have taken some. But I thought that in the desert we'd be drinking out of jerry cans; it never occurred to me that I might have to rely on the River Euphrates. Certainly we wouldn't risk drinking from wells: there seemed a good chance that wells might have been poisoned.

The atmosphere in the patrol remained tense

but cheerful. We kept asking for satellite pictures of the area where we were heading, and in the end some did arrive. They were of poor quality, but they suggested we were right to leave our vehicles behind, since they showed that the desert was extremely flat and open. What we didn't realize, because we weren't properly instructed about these particular images, was that we were reading the imagery upside-down, mistaking low ground for high ground, wadis for ridges and so on.

Our second departure was set for the evening of Tuesday 22 January 1991. Before we left, we had a big meal of fresh food. Then came last-minute checks as we went through all our pockets to make sure that we were carrying no scrap of paper that would give away who we were or where we came from. The only identification I had on me was a pair of metal discs slung on a chain round my neck. These bore my name, army number, blood group and religion (Church of England). To stop them clinking, I'd covered them in black masking tape. I'd taped a good-luck talisman on each disc. One was a new five-pence piece given to me by my mother-in-law, to accompany her Christmas present of a

Samurai sword (the Japanese reckon it's bad luck to give a sword without a coin). The other was a big old British penny which I'd found lying head-up in the sand of the training area near the camp at Victor. It must have been dropped there by a Brit many years earlier. I remembered the old saying: *See a penny, pick it up, all the day you'll have good luck*. I'm not really superstitious, but thought I might as well give myself any advantage I could.

This time all three Bravo patrols were deploying at the same time, in two Chinooks. Because we were sharing our air transport with half of Bravo Three Zero, and they were due to drop off first, we hauled our own gear to the front of the fuselage, leaving room for four guys, their kit and two Land Rovers at the back. The chopper was so full that the pilot had to taxi it like a fixed-wing aircraft in order to get it off the ground. Then, as he had it rolling, the tail came up a bit and we lifted away.

The noise in the back was horrendous: the roar of the engines, backed by the thudding of the rotor, made normal conversation impossible. But a few headsets, plugged into the intercom system, made it possible to listen to the pilots talking. When we landed to refuel at Arar, the pilot shut down his engines, and I sat there thinking, *I hope this thing doesn't start up again!* But when the refuelling was complete, the Chinook's engines re-started and off we went.

By then darkness had fallen, and we'd flown for only a few minutes when the pilot came on the intercom. 'Congratulations, guys,' he said. 'We've just crossed the border. You're now in Iraq.'

Great! I thought. *This is cool, flying three hundred kilometres into enemy territory. Nobody else is doing this. Nobody else knows we're going in.* But at the same time I was thinking, *This is real. This is dangerous.* During my time in the SAS I'd been in some hairy situations on missions in various parts of the world, and on military operations in Northern Ireland, but nothing as dramatic as this. This was the first time I'd been to war.

To keep under the radar, we were flying only ten or twenty metres off the ground. I took my hat off to the pilots, who were prepared to go into hostile airspace so lightly armed. Apart from our own weapons, the only armaments on board were two SA80 automatic rifles which the loadies could fire through the portholes. SA80s are poor-quality, unreliable weapons at the best of times. We'd told the pilots that if we were attacked when we landed, we would handle the firefight.

In my headphones I suddenly heard the pilot start shouting. A surface-to-air missile site had locked onto us. With such a heavy load, no violent evasive tactics were possible; he lowered the chopper and with great skill hovered less than a metre above the desert. He had chaff, which he could fire off if necessary to confuse incoming missiles, but I felt quite scared knowing that I wasn't in charge of my own destiny.

We seemed to hover for ever. I looked out through one of the portholes and was appalled to see how bright the moonlight was. The desert looked totally flat, without cover anywhere. Then after a minute or two we lifted again and carried on.

In my head I ran over the rations that I'd chosen and stowed in my bergen. I knew from experience that when you're sitting around in an OP, boredom makes you want to eat. But I'd restricted myself to a daily ration of one main meal, two packets of biscuits, and some fruit like pineapple or pears in syrup. The main meals were boil-in-the-bag – things like beef stew, chicken and pasta, pasta and meatballs, bacon and beans. They were pre-cooked and sealed in tough silver-foil sachets, which you could roll up and squash down.

As for personal kit, I was dressed, like the rest of the guys, in regular DPMs (disruptive pattern material combat fatigues). We'd also been issued with lightweight, sand-coloured desert smocks, which unbelievably dated from the Second World War. I had worked my silk escape map into the waistband that held the drawstring of my trousers, and taped the twenty gold sovereigns onto the inside of my belt. On my head I was wearing a German Army cap, and on my feet a pair of brown Raichle Gore-Tex-lined walking boots, with well-insulated uppers and soles. On my hands I had a pair of green aviator's gloves, made of fine leather. As useful extras I had two shamags. One was very light-coloured, like a biscuit. The other was thicker and altogether more suitable, being oatmeal and purple, with the design favoured by the special forces of Oman.

In my right arm I was cradling my chosen weapon, a 203, which I'd fitted with a makeshift sling made of nylon paracord. Four of the patrol had 203s, and the rest Minimis, depending on how much other weight they were carrying. Since the 203 weighs 10 lb and the Minimi 16 lb, those with less to carry had the machine guns. I, being the patrol medic and saddled with the 12 lb medical pack, had a 203, as did Legs Lane, who had the 30 lb radio. Stan, on the other hand, who was exceptionally strong, had a Minimi. On board the Chinook we kept the rifles loaded, with bullets up the spout and safety catches on, in case of sudden action.

Each of us also had a 66 rocket launcher – a simple, disposable American device that you throw away after firing. In its folded state it looks like a tube, with the rocket pre-packed inside it; you can carry it either slung over your shoulder on a strap or, as I had mine, laid across the top of my bergen, under the flap. When the time comes to fire, all you have to do is pull out the second half of the tube to make a longer barrel, flip up the sight and pull the trigger.

As the chopper clattered on through the night, I was trying to think ahead, mainly about escape and evasion. The Regiment's official line was that if the patrol was compromised, we should head back towards Saudi Arabia. But since Saudi would be nearly 300 kilometres off, and the Syrian border was only 130 kilometres to the west, we had already decided that if things went wrong, we'd leg it for Syria. That would make obvious sense. The Syrians had announced that if they picked up downed aircrew from any of the Allied nations, they would hand them back to the Coalition forces.

Talking it over at Al Jouf, we reckoned that we could jog and run to the border in two nights. But we'd forgotten about water: you can't jog carrying full jerry cans, and there was no other source around. Nor had we bargained for the cold.

Five minutes out from Bravo Three Zero's location, the loadie gave a thumbs-up signal. I smelled rather than heard the Land Rover engines start up. The back of the Chinook filled with choking diesel fumes.

Then two fingers from the loadie indicated 'Two minutes to landing'.

Then one minute.

With a bump, we were on the ground. The tailgate went down, the vehicles rolled, and the guys hurried out into the night. That was a tense moment, because it was perfectly possible that enemy were waiting to receive us. The rest of us were at the ready: we had our webbing on and weapons in hand. If the chopper had come under fire, we'd have burst out and gone to ground. But nothing happened. The tailgate came up. With some of the weight gone, the heli made a normal take-off, and we were away again.

Twenty minutes later it was our turn.

We grabbed our own kit and dragged it to the edge of the tailgate. Soon the loadie gave us five fingers, then two. We pulled on goggles to keep flying sand and grit out of our eyes. As the chopper hit the deck, the tailgate went down. Cold air and dust came screaming in, but thanks to the goggles I could still see.

We tumbled out, dragging our kit.

Above us was a horrendous sight. Two enormous blue lights seemed to be blazing above the aircraft. For a moment I couldn't think what was happening. Had we been caught by an Iraqi searchlight? Then I realized that the downdraught from the rotors was raising a storm of grit, and as the grains hit the whirling blades they lit up with a bright blue glow. *Somebody's bound to see this*, I thought.

While the noise of the Chinook's engines still covered us, the guys with machine guns snapped their belted magazines into place. Then in a few more seconds the heli lifted away into the night and was gone.

For the last couple of hours we'd been in deafening noise. Now suddenly we were thrown into silence. The air was still, the night clear. We lay facing outwards in a circle on the desert floor. Dogs barked not far off to the east. They'd heard us, even if nobody else had.

With our goggles off, we had a good view of our surroundings. We'd landed in the middle of a dry wadi maybe 200 metres wide. Scattered clouds were sailing across the moon, and in the clear intervals its light was very bright. Too bright. As our eyes adjusted, we could see that the wadi had walls five or ten metres high, apparently with a level plain above them on either side.

The main supply route was somewhere up ahead of us, to the north, running roughly east to west. The ground beneath us was dead flat, and consisted of hard-baked clay, but we found we were lying right between a set of tracks made by a vehicle whose tyres had sunk into the dry mud. I realized that the mud was only a few centimetres deep, and that under it lay solid rock. There was no loose material with which to fill our sandbags.

I reckoned that if any Iraqis had seen the chopper, they'd already be running or driving across the flats towards the lip of the wadi. I had visions of people coming from all directions and suddenly appearing on the rim, against the stars.

'Let's get some guns onto the high ground,' I whispered to Andy. So we sent out two lads, one on either side, to go up the wadi walls and keep a lookout.

Gradually the barking of dogs died away and left us in total silence. Our most urgent need was to get our kit out of sight. We began dragging it into the shadow of the moonlight cast by the right-hand or eastern wall. From the middle of the wadi that shadow looked solid and deep – a good place in which to hide. But when we reached it, we found it was an illusion. There was no cover of any kind, and in the daylight the whole river bed would be dangerously open.

In heaving and dragging our kit, we were leaving marks in the baked mud of the wadi floor. But we had a much bigger problem than that. There was hardly a grain of sand in the whole area. We were on bedrock. Training in the dunes of the Gulf, we had built beautiful OPs with the greatest of ease, digging into the sand and filling as many bags as we needed. Here, without sand, our bags were useless.

We needed to find out exactly where we were. So Mark got out a GPS unit and plotted our position to within a few metres. Then we pulled in our two flanking guys, who reported that the desert on either side of the wadi ran away level in flat plains, without a stitch of cover.

Andy went forward with Mark to recce the ground ahead. As the rest of us lay waiting for them to return, we began to realize how cold it was. The wind bit through our DPMs and smocks, which were far too light for the job, in both weight and colour. They gave very little protection against the cold, and were such a pale sandy colour that they shone like beacons in the moonlight – my builder had been right! Way down at Victor, several hundred miles further south, the nights had been warm and the days hot enough to make us sweat. Nobody had thought to warn us that things would be different up here.

The dogs started barking again. It was hard to tell what had set them off this time. Could they hear us, or was our scent carrying on the wind? We reckoned they were no more than 400 or 500 metres away.

That figured, because the satellite photos had shown irrigated fields and habitations within about that distance of our drop-off point. We just hoped they didn't come across to suss out what was disturbing them.

In twenty minutes Andy and Mark were back. 'Right,' Andy whispered. 'We'll head up here. Get forward up the wadi.'

Four of the guys struggled into their bergens and walked forward about 300 metres, then went to ground. As soon as they were settled, the rest of us moved up to join them. Then the first four went back and picked up the rest of their kit, including the jerry cans, which were tied together in pairs with tape. Once they'd joined us, we went back, and so it continued for most of the night: shuttling forward, back, forward, back. It was tiring work.

By 0500 we had moved about two kilometres to the north, and were in the area selected for the OP. The sky in the east was already beginning to lighten. We were still in the wadi, but we couldn't stay where we were, because the ground was far too open, and the walls were bare rock, so there was no chance of digging. Then Andy went on round a corner with Stan and found that the wadi came to a dead end in a cul-de-sac no bigger than a good-sized room. The walls were fairly steep, but on the left-hand side, as we faced north, one massive slab of rock had fallen off the side of the ravine. The detached lump was about two metres high, and lay a metre or so clear of the wall, with a second, smaller rock near its foot. It made some natural shelter. A little further to the south there was an overhang going back under the wall. The floor was of hard-baked clay, with loose rocks and some stunted thorn bushes scattered about.

It wasn't a great hiding place, but it was the best we could find.

CHAPTER 4
CONTACT!

We went into our hiding place and packed away all the kit for the OP, because it was no use to us in this rock desert. We put the jerry cans at the bottom, with the thermal sheets, cam nets and empty sandbags on top, to deaden any noise. Some of us sat on the cans, a couple of us tucked in underneath the overhang, and the rest settled around the rocks at various places. If we wanted to shift about, we went at a crouch or on hands and knees, but all movement was kept to a minimum.

The end of the wadi covered us from the north – the direction of the main supply route – and we were quite well protected by the sides. But to our rear we were dangerously exposed. If anyone came up the river bed, following our tracks, they'd be bound to walk or drive right on top of us.

'This is no good,' somebody muttered. 'If it looks bad in the daylight, we'll have to consider getting on the phone so we can be relocated.'

Before dawn, we put out two claymore mines, about fifty metres down the wadi with wires running back to our position, so that we could blow up anybody who approached along the foot of the eastern wall.

At first light Andy and I crept carefully up a small channel and lay at the top of the bank for a look around. Daybreak revealed that flat, grey-brown plains stretched away into the distance to the east and west. But there, straight ahead, only a couple of hundred metres away, was the main supply route. It ran right and left across our front on a big embankment like a long ridge. To the left, one harmless-looking civilian truck was parked on the edge of the highway. It had an open back and slatted sides, as if it was used for carrying animals. One or two other lorries rumbled along the road.

On the high ground to our right, another couple of hundred metres away, was something much more sinister: an anti-aircraft position. Through our binoculars we could see the twin barrels of guns, which we identified from our manual as SA60s, poking up above the emplacement. There were at least two Iraqis moving about.

The sight gave us a nasty fright. Those guns could only be there to protect some installation from air attack. It meant we were right on the edge of an enemy position. We would have to be extremely careful.

We came back down and let the rest of the guys know that there were enemy within 400 metres of us. In the shelter of the wadi we heard the occasional vehicle go along the road, but we kept our heads down while we considered what to do. It was too dangerous to spend any length of time where we were. We had to get a message through to base, asking for a relocation or a return.

The trouble was, the 319 radio did not seem to be working. It should have been possible for us to communicate instantly with the base station in Cyprus, and from there messages should have been back in Al Jouf within a couple of minutes. But although Legs patiently tried different frequencies and experimented with various aerial arrays, he got no response. (We discovered much later that we'd been given the wrong frequencies.) For the moment there was no serious worry, because we knew that as a fall-back we had the Lost Comms procedure. This meant that if we had not come on air within forty-eight hours, a helicopter would automatically return, either bringing us a new radio set or armed with a plan to shift us elsewhere.

We took turns to go on lookout duty, or 'stag', while the others had a meal or a sleep. We did an hour's guard-duty each, holding the clackers for detonating the claymores and watching the wadi. The rest of the guys, having had a sleepless night, were glad to get their heads down. It was so cold that several of them struggled into their NBC suits and lay around in them. We were all more or less hidden, and there was a good chance that if we kept still, even a man looking up the wadi from a distance would not have seen us.

Then, late in the afternoon, we heard voices. A boy began calling out, and a man answered him. Peering cautiously over the western rim, we saw them driving a herd of goats. They were walking across the plain, nearly parallel to the wadi, but heading in towards us as they moved northwards, and calling the goats on as they went. The truck with slatted sides was still parked on the far side of the main supply route. It looked as if the goatherds had come out to check their flock, or were about to load the animals up.

Either way, they were too close for comfort. We grabbed our weapons and lay like stones, hardly breathing, each man with a round up the spout.

From the jingling of the goat bells and the voices, we reckoned the flock passed within fifty metres of our hiding place. As the sounds faded into the distance, we kept still, listening. Half an hour later, we crept to the top of the bank again to check what was happening: the truck had disappeared, and there was no sign of the goats. But where they had gone, we couldn't tell.

This place was bad news. There was so much activity in the area that it could only be a matter of time before we were compromised.

There was still no response on the radio, and we began to grow nervous. We were also getting frozen. I had the best boots of anyone in the patrol, but even I had numb feet. Oddly enough, I didn't feel hungry, and all I ate during the day was a bar of chocolate and a packet of biscuits.

As soon as it got dark, Andy, Mark, Stan and Dinger decided to take a look around.

'We'll leave in this direction,' Andy briefed the rest of us in whispers, 'and we'll come back in the same way. The pass number's the sum of nine.'

This meant that when they returned, one of us would state a number between one and eight. The correct response would be the number which, added to the original number, made nine. So, if we said 'three', they would have to reply 'six'. In hindsight, this was a bit stupid. If anyone other than the patrol had approached us, it would have been an Iraqi, and just by speaking to them we would be immediately compromised.

'We shouldn't be more than three or four hours,' Andy continued. 'As we come in, the first man will walk down with his arms extended and his weapon held out sideways in his right hand.'

If the rest of us heard a contact, he went on, we were to stand-to, wait five or six minutes for the recce group to come through our position, and put fire down on anyone following them. If our own four guys didn't appear, we were to make for the drop-off point, and they would join us there.

They left at 2300 while the rest of us took

turns to do an hour's stag. Not a sound broke the silence; the night was utterly still, but not nearly so light as the one before, because the sky was full of clouds.

The recce party returned safely at 0330. They had found that the main supply route was not a metalled road, but just a series of dirt tracks running parallel through the desert; the tracks spread out across nearly a kilometre. They'd also discovered a single white post standing in the ground, about 300 metres from the lying-up position, but they could not make out what it was marking. Then they'd checked out a little tented encampment beyond the spot on which the truck we'd seen had been parked. It was a second anti-aircraft position, with a few vehicles parked around it.

For what was left of the night they got their heads down, and the rest of us stagged on again. When morning came, we decided it was too dicey to stay. There were too many people about, and we were too close to the site that the anti-aircraft guns were guarding.

For the rest of the second day we tried to get through on the radio, but no luck. We also tried using our Satcom telephone. We didn't want to speak for long on it, because any call that lasted more than twenty seconds could be picked up by direction-finding apparatus. So we switched the set to listening-wait, hoping to hear a call from base. Then occasionally we would come up on the call-sign with a quick request for a comms check: 'Hello Zero Alpha, this is Bravo Two Zero, radio check, over.' But nothing happened.

It looked as though we were going to have to rely on our Lost Comms procedure. That would mean pulling back down the wadi to the drop-off point, and being there when the chopper came in at midnight – forty-eight hours after dropping us off. We hoped that it would take us somewhere better, but more likely it would just bring us a new radio. Either way, after dark the whole patrol was going to move back, humping all our kit. We weren't looking forward to making the effort.

It was about four o'clock in the afternoon that everything started to go wrong.

Once again we heard the herder boy calling his goats. This time he sounded closer, and coming directly towards us. I'd been talking to Andy and Dinger about the radio, and I was under the overhang when the boy started shouting, from a point directly above my head, but some way out behind me.

The three of us lay still, but when I looked across at Vince, on the other side of the rock, he was craning his head to see if he could spot the boy. Mouthing at him furiously, and giving tiny, frantic movements of our fingers, we tried to make him keep his head down.

If we'd all stayed still, we might have been OK. Nine times out of ten, if hidden people don't move, they get away with it. What betrays them is shape, shadow, shine and, above all, movement. It's the same with birds and animals in a wood: as long as they keep still, you don't see them, but the instant one moves, that's it.

But Vince moved. Wanting to see what was happening, he eased his head up until the boy could have caught sight of him.

The shouting stopped. There was no cry of alarm, but the sudden silence was ominous. It was pretty obvious that the boy had run off. I crawled round to Vince and hissed, 'Did he see you?'

'No, no, no,' he answered. 'We're OK.'

I left it at that, but I didn't believe him. Things were getting scary: we were about to be rumbled. I felt fear starting up in my stomach. Legs was still at the radio, trying to get through. 'Have you been on the guard net?' I asked him.

'No.'

'Well, get on it and start tapping Morse.' The guard net sends out new frequencies, and can only be used in an emergency. This was one.

Legs started working out his Morse code message: *High possibility compromise. Request relocation or expel*. But just as he was tapping it in, we heard the roar of a heavy engine and the squealing and grinding of what we thought were tank-tracks, approaching up the wadi.

Wild thoughts raced through my mind: an anti-personnel round from a tank could destroy us all.

'Get the sixty-sixes open,' somebody shouted, and we pulled open the tubes and cocked the disposable rocket launchers. The guys had spread out round the end of the wadi, lying behind whatever cover they could find.

Every second the rattling noise of the tracks got louder. We were stuck, pinned like rats in the dead end of the ravine, just waiting for the tank to come round the corner. We couldn't tell what else might also be coming at us over the flat ground above. The chances were that the Iraqis were deploying behind us too; even at that moment, they were probably advancing on our position. A couple of hand grenades tossed over the edge would make a nice mess of us. Even so, if the tank came into view and levelled its gun on us, we'd have no option but to run up onto the plain and chance it with the anti-aircraft positions on the high ground.

By now it was 1700 hours, but still full daylight. We started drinking, because we knew that if we had to run for it in the desert, we'd need the liquid inside us. Other guys began frantically repacking their kit, pulling off the warm jackets they'd been wearing and stuffing them into their bergens. A couple of the lads struggled out of their NBC suits and stowed them.

I checked my 203 magazines again. Each could hold thirty rounds, but I'd only loaded them with twenty-eight, to leave the springs a bit looser and cut down the chance of a stoppage. The spares were in my left-hand lower pouch.

Then, suddenly, something did come round the corner.

Not a tank . . . but a yellow bulldozer.

The driver had the blade high up in front of him,

obviously using it as a shield. We all kept still, lying or crouching in firing positions, but we knew the man had seen us. He was only 150 metres away when he stopped, stared, and reversed out of sight before trying to turn round. Obviously a local, he must have known that the wadi came to a dead end, and his only purpose in coming up it had been to find out who or what was in there. We held our breath as the screeching and crunching gradually died away.

For a minute or two we felt more relief than anything else. But we felt certain that the local militia must be deploying behind us, and we needed to get out of there. We'd already decided to ditch the surplus kit we couldn't carry, but we stowed the 66s away, pulled our bergens on and were ready for the off. As we were about to leave, I called, 'Get your shamags round your heads.' So we all wrapped our heads in shawls, in case we could bluff our way and pass as Arab soldiers, even for a few minutes.

We started walking southwards, down the wadi, towards our emergency rendezvous point. Finding myself at the front, I led the patrol out, my 203 locked and loaded, ready for action. Andy was in the middle, the normal slot for a patrol commander.

Dusk was already coming on, and I was hoping we could reach the drop-off point, less than two kilometres to the south, and put down enough fire to defend ourselves until dark. Then we'd have to wait until the chopper came in.

Moving out, I kept close in to the left-hand wall of the wadi, because that was the steepest, and in the lee of it we were out of sight of the AA guns. When I turned round, I found that the guys had opened up to a tactical spacing of maybe twenty metres between each; but I was thinking, *If we have a nonsense here, we want to be tight together*. So I yelled back, 'Close up!'

The bulldozer had gone out of sight, but we were moving towards where we'd last seen it. All too soon the wadi began to flatten out, and on our left a long slope ran up to the plain above. As we came clear of the steep part of the wadi wall, I suddenly saw two Iraqis on the high ground above us, guns down by their sides. They were barely 200 metres away, and weren't moving. They didn't look surprised as we walked into their view. Both were wearing dark overcoats on top of their dishdashes (native cotton robes), which reached down to their ankles. Also they had red-and-white shamags done up on top of their heads like turbans. I reckoned they were civilians or possibly militia.

It's that boy, I said to myself. *He's tipped them off.*

We kept going. But the two Iraqis began to parallel us, moving forward. In case anybody hadn't seen them, I called back, 'We've got two on the high ground to the left, and they're walking down. Keep going!'

Afterwards, I realized that the two Iraqis were waiting for reinforcements to come up; also, they were probably a bit confused because they didn't know who we were. But at the time I was wondering if we could outrun them, or lose them somehow, without starting a firefight.

Then I blew it in a big way. *I'm going to try the double bluff here*, I thought, and I waved at them.

Unfortunately I did it with my left hand, which to an Arab is the ultimate insult – your left hand being the one you wipe your bum with. Immediately one of them brought up his weapon and opened fire.

Contact!

We swung round and put a couple of short bursts back at them. Both dropped onto one knee to continue firing. As I stood there, I saw Vince take off down the wadi.

'Stay together!' I yelled. 'Slow down!'

We began to run, turning to fire aimed bursts. The secret is to keep them short – no more than two or three rounds at a time. Otherwise the recoil makes the weapon drift up and the rounds go high. We ran and fired, ran and fired.

Within seconds a tipper truck with metal sides screeched to a halt beside the two Iraqis, and eight or ten guys spilled out of it. Stan also saw an armoured car carrying a .50 machine gun pull up. Some of the Iraqis began firing from the back of the truck, others from positions behind it.

It looked as though there were about a dozen men altogether. They had automatic rifles and at least the one heavy machine gun. But their fire was inaccurate, and we could cope with them. In my mind they weren't the real threat. I was more worried that a bigger force was probably driving round ahead of us – out of sight – to cut off our retreat.

Looking back, I found that the guys were running across the open ground, struggling under the weight of their bergens. At one moment the patrol formed a tight group, then we spread out again, some running, others taking turns to stop, put down rounds, then run again.

If anyone says he's not frightened in a firefight, I don't believe him. I was certainly scared, and so was everyone else. But the Regiment's strength lies in the fact that its members are highly trained to control their fear and respond positively to any threat they face.

In this contact, the flow of adrenalin was fearsome. On we went, legging it up the slope now, shooting at the enemy as they ran back and forth between vehicles. Three times I saw men go down when I fired. One went down behind a mound and never came up. Two others rolled over as they were running. At one point there was a massive explosion from one of the vehicles.

Green tracer started coming across, whizzing past our heads. We were right in the open, and whenever one of us stopped to turn and fire, the enemy seemed to concentrate on him, and we could see the tracer close in on the stationary target.

As the tracer flew, I started screaming into my tactical rescue beacon (TACBE) – a device that sends a distress signal to any nearby friendly aircraft, and which can also be used on voice comms:

'TURBO! TURBO! This is Bravo Two Zero. CONTACT! CONTACT!'

Andy was doing the same. The TACBEs should have produced an answer within seconds. But nothing happened.

'My TACBE's broken!' I yelled to Andy.

'Can't get through on mine, either.'

'Keep trying.'

Then somebody shouted, 'I'm ditching my bergen!'

Someone else yelled, 'I am too!'

Next second, I was doing it myself, fighting to get the straps off my shoulder. Then I was kneeling by the pack, struggling with the clips on the top flap to free my 66. I got one clip undone. Just as I reached my hand towards the other, the clip exploded in pieces, hit by a .50 bullet. If my hand had been three or four centimetres farther forward, I would have lost it. The heavy round put the bergen down flat beside me. I leaped on it, grabbed the 66, whipped it over my shoulder and started off again. Ahead of me to the right I saw big splashes of soil or rock coming up. The anti-aircraft position had opened up on us, and rounds from those things were coming across as well.

By now we were walking. We couldn't run uphill any more. But as I moved away from my bergen, I was thinking, *What is there in there that I should have?* Then I realized: it was the medic pack. 'Left behind the medic pack!' I shouted to no one in particular.

When I'd gone about twenty metres from the bergen I said to Legs, 'Have you got the radio?'

'No,' he gasped. 'No time. I had to leave it.'

Suddenly I remembered, *My hip flask!* It was the one my wife had given me for Christmas, and it was still in my bergen.

I don't know what happened. The sensible thing would have been to leave it behind. But something clicked, and without hesitation I ran back down the slope. As I reached the bergen, I thought, *You idiot, you're going to get shot now.* As I bent down, my back to the Iraqis, I imagined parts of my chest hurtling out in front of me, and wondered what it would look like. Would my clothes tear apart and bits of flesh and bone fly out? But I stuck my hand into the top of the pack, found the flask, brought it out, stuffed it into a trouser pocket and started forward again.

By then I was finding it hard to walk. I felt

like I was suffocating. But fear was driving me on.

At last we got over the top, into dead ground, and collapsed onto the deck. 'I don't know how we managed that,' Andy gasped.

'Nor do I,' I said. 'But look at this – at least I got my flask back.'

'Where was it?'

'In my bergen,' I told him. Andy was stunned. 'I went back for it.' I unscrewed the top, took a swig of whisky and handed it to him.

For a few seconds we lay there, trying to get our breath. When we stood up again to see where the guys were, we were amazed to find everyone in one piece. I'd thought we must have lost two or three, but they all appeared and came round, just like that, nobody so much as touched.

It took us only a few seconds to reach a group decision. If our Lost Comms procedure worked, the Chinook would come in to the drop-off point at midnight; but now that we'd stirred up such a hornets' nest, and the Iraqis knew we were in the area, the chances were that they'd ambush the helicopter and shoot it down.

We decided it was safer to make for the Syrian border.

First, though, we'd head south, to throw the Iraqis off our track.

'Right,' I called, 'let's go.' Without trying to take command, but wanting out of this place, I led off, with Andy behind me and the rest in line.

By then we thought we were out of range of the Iraqis' original position, but some of them had worked their way round onto a closer ridge. As we came into view they opened up again. Also, we were back in view of the anti-aircraft gunners, who resumed firing. Some rounds were whizzing past us, others landing ten or fifteen metres away. We just kept walking like mad.

Then the vehicle with the .50 machine gun came up onto a crest and started cracking rounds over us again from a range of 400 or 500 metres. Luckily for us, though, the light was dying and the rounds were going far too high.

So we set off, and walked for our lives into the gathering night.

CHAPTER 5
DISASTER STRIKES

Thursday 24 January: Escape – Night One

Until we cleared the second long valley, a few anti-aircraft rounds were still falling in. Some burst in the air with a puff of black smoke and a crack, and others hit the ground. Then we were in the clear, out on the barren gravel plains, and we headed due south, marching as fast as we could in single file. Mark guided us with his GPS.

It was a great shock to us that we seemed to have been abandoned by our own people. It's an unwritten rule of the Regiment that if guys need help, their mates come and get them. Now we'd yelled ourselves hoarse on radios and TACBEs, and there had been no result. We could not have known at the time that the nearest aircraft that could have detected the TACBE was 500 kilometres to the east – about four times the maximum range of the machines – and that we had been given the wrong radio frequencies, so that none of our calls on the 319 had gone through unscrambled.

After half an hour someone shouted, 'We're being followed!'

Looking back, we saw the lights of a vehicle. At first we couldn't tell whether or not it was moving, but then through Vince's night-sight we made out that it was definitely coming after us. In some places the desert was completely flat, with no features of any kind. The vehicle could make good speed across those areas. But luckily for us there were also a lot of wadis, in which the going was rough and the driver had to go slowly. There was no way he could see us – the night was too dark for that – but he knew the line we'd taken down the first wadi. He was driving in the direction he'd seen us go.

Our boots crunched on the ground. We could have been quieter if we'd gone slowly, but we needed speed. I went as fast as I could in spite of the noise, with the other guys close behind, at intervals of no more than two metres between each man. We knew that although the desert seemed empty, there were outposts dotted all over it. We could have walked onto a position at any moment. There was also the risk of stumbling into an encampment of the desert-dwelling Bedouin.

After an hour, and maybe eight or nine kilometres, we stopped and came together in a group. Dinger took off his jacket and started covering it with rocks.

'What are you doing?' I asked.

'I'm ditching my jacket. It's far too hot.'

'Keep it,' I told him. 'Tie it round your waist. You're going to need it.'

Later he thanked me, and said I'd saved his life. But for the moment he cursed as we got going again. I kept thinking of all the stuff I'd left behind. I hated the idea of the Iraqis stealing our kit. With a flicker of satisfaction I remembered that we'd left the claymores and anti-personnel mines buried in the floor of the wadi, and wondered whether they'd taken any of the enemy out. I also wished I'd kept more food in my pouches, and less ammunition. As it was, I had nothing to eat but two packets of hard, biscuits, five in each packet. At the very least we were in for forty-eight hours of hard going, on little food and water.

When you're moving in a straight line, and have a contact, it's usually the Number One who gets hit. Even if he isn't shot, it's Numbers Two and Three who have to get him out of trouble. On that march our standard operating procedure (SOP) – which everyone knew by heart – was that if we hit trouble the lead scout would put a 203 round towards the enemy and empty a magazine in their direction. By that time Two and Three should already have gone to ground, and be putting rounds down. Number One would then spring back, zigzagging, and go to ground himself, to cover the other two, while the rest of the guys fanned out. It was important, though, not to panic and start firing at phantoms, as shots would immediately give our position away.

I was Number One. Vince, who was Number Two, kept dropping back, as if he didn't want to be near me. 'If we get a contact in front,' he said, 'whatever you do, don't fire back. You're better off sticking your hands up.'

I said, 'Hey – if we get a contact, I'm shooting. Because if we get captured, we'll get done.'

'Don't. If you shoot one of them, they'll kill the lot of us.'

By that time the patrol had closed up again, and there was a bit of an argument. Nobody agreed with Vince so I just said, 'Stick behind me,' and led off again.

A few minutes later a message came up the line, to slow down and stop. Somebody shouted, 'Stan's gone down!'

Stan was one of the strongest guys in the patrol. I ran back and asked what was wrong, but he was on the deck and seemed to be nearly unconscious.

'Stan!' I said. 'What's wrong?'

He just went 'Urrrhhh!'

One of the guys said, 'I reckon it's heat exhaustion. He's sweating really badly.'

'But it's freezing,' I said.

I'd been sweating a bit myself, but not that much. What we didn't know was that Stan was still wearing his thermal underclothes under his DPMs. He'd been caught out with them on when the contact started, and hadn't had a chance to take them off. The result was that he'd become seriously overheated and had sweated himself dry.

We got out our water bottles. I tipped sachets of white rehydrate powder into four of them and started pouring the water down his neck. He drank six pints at least. That should have pulled him round, but he was still dizzy and exhausted, not making much sense.

Somebody said, 'We should look for a safe spot and leave him. Find a hole in the ground, somewhere we can find him again when we get reinforcements.'

There was no way I'd do that. We couldn't leave one guy by himself – not when there were seven more of us, all strong and still fresh. But if he thought we'd ditch him, maybe it would spur him on. I bent over Stan and said in a menacing voice, 'Listen: if you don't start walking, we're going to leave you. Understand?'

He nodded and gave a grunt.

'Get up, then,' I told him. 'Just fix your eyes on my webbing, and keep that in sight.'

Andy took Stan's Minimi, then said to me, 'Chris, take this,' and gave me the night-sight Stan had been carrying slung round his neck.

'I don't want that,' I protested. The sight weighed about two kilograms, and I thought it would be a pain to have it dangling on my chest. But I took it – and thank God I did, because without doubt it saved my life. I also took a box of 200 rounds for the Minimi and slung it over my shoulder.

We couldn't hang around any longer, because the vehicle lights were still bobbing about in the darkness behind us. I got hold of Stan again and repeated, 'Just walk behind me – and whatever you do, keep going.'

Once more I led, with Stan at my back now, Vince behind him, and the rest of the patrol following. Lead scout is a tiring job, because you have to be looking ahead all the time; but, being quite observant, I reckoned that if there was something in front of us, I would see it as quickly as anyone else. As before, Andy took the patrol commander's middle slot.

Every time we stopped for Mark to do a GPS check, I'd say, 'Stan, get your head down for a minute,' and he'd lie down without a word. When we were ready to start again I'd give him a kick and say, 'OK, Stan, let's go,' and he'd get up again and start walking right behind me – only to fall back, farther and farther.

The vehicle lights were still coming up behind us. We decided to double back on ourselves. Until then we'd been heading back towards the Saudi border. Now we resolved to turn right – westwards – for a spell, then right again, and head northwards across the main supply route which we'd been watching. The loss of our jerry cans had forced us to modify our original plan of going north-west, straight for the Syrian border. Obviously we would need water, so we decided to aim due north, for the River Euphrates, and follow it out to the frontier.

So, after sixteen quick kilometres southwards, we turned due west and did ten kilometres in that direction. The pace was very, very fast – speed marching, probably about nine kilometres an hour. Now and then we crossed a dry wadi like the one in which we'd lain up, but for most of the way the desert was completely open. Whenever we heard the sound of jet engines overhead, we'd switch on our TACBEs and shout into them. But there was no answer.

By the end of the ten kilometres westwards, the

strain was starting to tell. We'd been moving at high speed, with 20 kg belt-kits and our weapons, and we were sweating quite a bit in spite of the cold. That meant we were all thirsty, and soon we'd drunk nearly all our water. Whenever we stopped, we made sure to get more liquid down Stan's neck. He had kept going by sheer willpower. After such a collapse it was a major feat to maintain the pace we were setting.

As soon as we'd fully lost sight of the vehicle behind us, we made our second right turn and headed north, stopping frequently to check our position with the GPS. This went on until we thought we were back within about seven kilometres of the main supply route. We were coming to the most dangerous bit. If we got caught on those tracks, out in the open, it would all be over. We needed to move even more quickly.

By then I was using the night-sight most of the time, with my weapon tucked under my left arm. It was awkward and tiring to walk like that. After a while my eyes started to hurt as well, because looking through the sight was like staring at a light. But there was no alternative. Soon I could make out the ridge on which the anti-aircraft guns were mounted, and I kept scanning for lights or artificial shapes, focusing my attention on what lay ahead.

Disaster hit us without warning.

We arrived at the main supply route and started to cross the tracks. There were about a dozen of them, running side by side, marked in hard mud, and they seemed to be spread over 200 or 300 metres. Out on that open expanse I felt very exposed, so I turned up the pace even faster. Then, just short of the high ground, I looked through the night-sight yet again and saw a black object that I thought might be a building or vehicle. At the foot of the slope I stopped to confer with Andy.

But Andy wasn't there.

I saw Stan behind me, with his head hanging down, then Vince . . . but no one else.

'Where's the rest of the patrol?' I demanded.

'I don't know,' said Vince. 'We've lost them.'

'What d'you mean, *lost them*?'

'They split off somewhere.'

Vince didn't seem too concerned, but I was on the verge of panic. 'Right,' I said. 'Let's get up on the high ground, fast.' I took one more look at the black object, decided it was a rock, and hustled forward as fast as I could. Just short of the top of the ridge I stopped again. Stan lay down like he was dead. Vince was completely zonked as well – he just sat there and couldn't speak.

It had been at least an hour since I'd last spoken to Andy – so it could have been that long since the patrol had split. Looking back across the open gravel plains with the night-sight, I had a clear view for miles. It seemed impossible that the others could have gone far enough to vanish. I kept scanning and thinking that at any second I would see five black figures trudging in single file. I saw nothing.

For a few moments I was dumbfounded. Then I thought, *My TACBE and Andy's are compatible; if both are switched on at the same time, we should be able to talk to each other*. The SOP for this situation was that anyone in difficulties would listen out on every hour and half-hour; so I waited five minutes till midnight, pressed the button and called: 'Andy! Andy!' No answer. I kept on for five minutes, fully expecting him to shout back, but no call came.

Things were going from bad to worse.

We were down to three men; one of them was out of the game, and the other didn't want to be in it.

I had my 66 and a few grenades in my belt-kit,

but otherwise we had only two main weapons: I had my 203, and Vince a 203 and a pistol. Stan had nothing but a bayonet.

Stan had drunk all my water and we also no longer had the GPS, which was with Mark. From now on we'd have to navigate by map, compass and dead reckoning – and this depended on knowing how fast we were covering the ground. The more tired we became, the less accurate we'd be. I regretted never having done a course in astral navigation: I could recognize the Plough, Orion's Belt and a few other constellations, but that was all.

I looked around. Stan was asleep on the ground beside me, but Vince had moved off about fifteen metres and was burying his ammunition – a box of 200 rounds and a sleeve of 203 grenades.

'What are you doing?' I hissed.

'I'm not carrying that stuff,' he said. 'It's too heavy. If we get into a big contact, we'll all be wasted anyway.'

'You've got to carry it,' I told him.

'I can't.'

'Give us those rounds here, then.'

I was fuming. We only had the two weapons, and might really need the ammunition. But I couldn't order Vince to carry it. So I slung the 203 bandolier over my shoulder and let him bury the box.

I went back, sat down, and waited until 0030. Then on the half-hour I tried the TACBE again. Still no reply.

We couldn't just sit where we were, so we cracked on again, with Stan just behind me and Vince at the back. We kept going until 0500, by which time I could feel blisters starting on my feet and we were all at the end of our tether. That was hardly surprising, as we'd covered the best part of seventy kilometres during the night.

Dawn wasn't far off. We needed somewhere to hole up for the day and we came across an old tank berm. This was a bank of soil about two metres high, built in the shape of a big U with one end open. A tank could drive into it and be hidden from the other three sides. Just short of it, and leading into it, were two tracks about twenty centimetres wide and ten deep, where a tank had sunk into the ground on its way in or out.

There was no point lying up inside the berm itself. The wind was blowing straight into its wide, open end so that its walls gave no shelter and anyone passing could look in. Equally, we couldn't lie outside the walls in the lee of the wind, because we'd have been in full view from the other direction. The only shelter from the wind, and at the same time cover from view, was in the tank-ruts outside.

'We're going to have to stay here,' I said, and we lay down in the deepest part of one of the tracks, head to toe. Vince was at one end, I was in the middle and Stan was beyond me. Down flat, we were more or less hidden, but I only had to raise my head a few centimetres to see out. It wasn't a great place to hide, because if anyone came to visit the berm for any reason, we would be compromised.

While we'd been on the move, the wind hadn't seemed too cold; but now that we'd stopped, it cut through our thin clothes. That was bad enough, but when daybreak came, the first thing I saw was heavy clouds piling in from the west.

Then I looked in the other direction and saw something square, about 600 metres off. It was either a little building or a vehicle, with antennae poking up out of it, and at least two men around it. This showed how right we'd been to remain alert during the night: here was some small military outpost, miles from anywhere – exactly the sort of place we might have walked onto.

We were separated from the rest of the unit.

We had barely any cover.

We could be discovered at any time.

The elements were against us.

But we had to spend the hours of daylight in this shallow ditch if we wanted any chance of escaping.

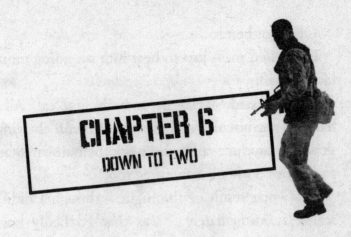

CHAPTER 6
DOWN TO TWO

Friday 25 January: Escape – Day Two

It was so cold. The wind came knifing through my DPMs and smock, so I opened my canvas map case and laid it over my legs. I wrapped one shamag round my head, and pulled the other round my shoulders. Even then I was still freezing. But somehow I must have dozed off, because I woke up shaking violently, with what felt like pins and needles in my face. When I opened my eyes, I couldn't believe it: it was snowing, and we were covered in white.

'Look at this!' I exclaimed bitterly. 'You'd think we were at the North Pole.' Nobody answered, so I said, 'Vince, are you all right?'

He grunted something back.

'Stan, how are you feeling?'

'Oh, a lot better.'

That lifted me – just to hear him sounding more like himself.

'Good,' I said. 'Well – get something to eat.' All I had was my biscuits, so I ate two of them, chewing slowly to produce saliva and work them down. Stan and Vince both ate something too.

The worst result of the night – though I didn't realize it immediately – was that I'd badly hurt my feet. The problem was my socks. They were made of rough grey-brown wool, and because our build-up had been done in such a rush, I'd worn them for four or five days on end before the deployment. By the time we started walking, they were already stiff with sand, dust and sweat – and now, as a result, they'd chewed the sides of my feet into large blisters.

The normal treatment – which we'd used on selection courses – would have been to push a needle into each blister, extract the fluid and inject tinc benzine, or Friar's Balsam. The process felt as if a red-hot poker had been laid against your foot, but it toughened the underlying skin enough for you to be able to walk on it. Even washing my feet and putting on plasters would have helped. But there, trapped in the tank-track, I couldn't even take my boots off to inspect the damage, let alone do anything to repair it.

Now and then during the day we saw military-looking vehicles driving in the distance. The snow turned to rain, then back to snow. Our ditch filled with water. The water dissolved the earth into mud, and soon we were wallowing in an icy quagmire. There was mud all over us, over our weapons. But all we could do was lie there in it.

I'd often been cold before, but never as cold as that. I became so frozen that I didn't even want to move my arm so that I could see my watch, and I asked Stan what the time was. 'Twelve o'clock,' was the answer. Was this day ever going to end?

In the tank-ruts, it was impossible to concentrate on anything for long, the discomfort was so intense. The only plus was that Stan seemed to be back to his normal spirits. He'd brought a proper boil-in-the-bag meal in his belt-kit, and once he'd got that down him, he was ready to go. Vince, on the other hand, was feeling the cold the worst of any of us. He wasn't whingeing, but he kept saying, 'Chris, I can't feel my fingers. I'm freezing.'

'So am I,' I told him. 'But we can't do anything,

Vince. We can't move, so we've just got to stick it out.'

'Can't we cuddle in together?' Sharing body heat to stave off hypothermia was a good idea but it wasn't possible right now.

'Not yet. It's too dangerous to move.'

The temptation to get up and go, to start moving again, was colossal: anything would be better than enduring this agony. But one of the Regiment's most basic SOPs is that during escape and evasion you don't move in daylight. If we were spotted walking, Iraqis would come at us from all sides. Grim as it was, I knew we should stay where we were.

Then, late in the afternoon, Vince worried me by saying, 'Look – I'm going down here.'

We had to do something. We had to take the risk.

'What's the time, Stan?'

'Four o'clock.'

'Let's cuddle in, then.'

Vince and I wriggled further down to where Stan lay, where the track was a bit wider. At that point we were all coming out into the open, but we accepted the danger and lay together, cuddling in for warmth, with me in the middle and the other two on the outsides.

After what seemed an age, I asked again, 'What's the time, Stan?'

'Five past four.'

This was real torture. It seemed like an eternity, lying there caked in freezing mud, with icy water soaking through our clothes. Whenever the snow stopped, the wind would get up and bring on the rain, and then the snow would start again . . .

Friday 25 January: Escape – Night Two

At last, at about five-thirty, darkness began to fall, and we decided to crawl inside the berm so that we could shift around and get some feeling back into our bodies. But until we tried to move, we didn't realize what a state we were in.

My fingers and toes were numb, but that was to be expected. It was when I went to stand up that I really got it: the pain in my knees and back was outrageous. I felt as if I had acute arthritis in my spine and hips. For a moment I was hit by despair.

We dragged ourselves inside the berm and tried to run around, to start the energy going and get some heat moving inside our bodies. But my feet were still numb, and clay had built up on the soles of my boots so I could hardly make any progress. Our hands were so dead that we couldn't even pick up our weapons – but luckily they had slings, so we ducked down, put our heads through the slings and stood up.

As Vince did so, he said, 'Chris – I can't carry my weapon. I just can't.'

I heard the note of desperation in his voice, so I just said quietly, 'Stan, you take it for him.' Stan took Vince's 203, leaving him with his pistol.

My memories of the next few hours are hazy, because I was being hit by hypothermia. All three of us were. But even though my mind was becoming clouded, I knew we had to keep moving.

'Right, fellers,' I said. 'We're going to have to start off again.' So away we went. I was stumbling with my weapon slung over my shoulder and my hands tucked under my arms, trying to get some feeling back into them. I kept thinking, *If we have a contact, we're done for, because we won't be able to shoot back*. I couldn't have pulled the trigger or changed magazines to save my life.

Then the clouds thickened up. Another flurry

of snow drove into our faces, hurtling in from the north-west, and soon we were tabbing over ground as white as on a Christmas card. The blizzard hid us, but we were blinded too and could easily walk onto an enemy position without spotting it.

When the moon came out again, the desert was light as day, and I could read my map without the torch. Vince, who kept falling behind, called, 'Hey, you're going to have to slow down. I need a rest.' Vince was highly-trained, fit, professional and very tough – but the cold was clearly hitting him harder than either Stan or myself.

'Vince,' I reminded him, 'you can't rest. We've got to keep moving, see if we can warm ourselves up.'

But although we were walking hard, we weren't getting any less cold. Normally, after you've walked for an hour, your circulation's really going, and you're warm all over. But because our clothes were soaked through, and this bitter wind was blowing, the chill-factor was keeping our body temperature right down. Also, there was no fuel left in me to re-stoke the fires: I'd burned it all up.

I knew that in our state, without warm clothes or shelter or food, we couldn't survive much longer. In fact, I thought it was likely we would all die that night. I'd never experienced such pain from the cold. In the course of training I'd had plenty of lectures on hypothermia, and now I recognized some of the symptoms in myself: disorientation, dizziness, sudden mood swings, outbursts of anger, confusion, drowsiness. Normally a man in that state would be put into a sleeping bag or a space blanket and brought round – but there was no chance of that out here.

So we kept walking – until Vince really started going down. 'Wait for me,' he called. 'You've got to wait . . .'

We did wait a few times. But then I decided that shock tactics were necessary. I knew that at home he had two young girls and a little baby, and that he was nuts about his family. So I gripped him by the arm and said, 'Vince, if you don't keep going, you're never going to see your kids again. Think about your home. Think how they'll want you back. Now – get your finger out and start moving.'

'Listen,' he said, 'I want to go to sleep. I'm too tired. I've got to sit down.'

'Vince, we can't sit down. If we stop, we're going to die. Get that? If we lie down and sleep, we'll freeze to death, and never know anything about it.'

We carried on walking for a bit, and then he shouted at me, 'Chris!'

'What?'

'My hands have gone black.'

My first thought was: *frostbite*. My own fingers were still numb, and I wondered what state my hands were in under my gloves. I walked back to Vince and found him staring down at his hands. He was wearing black leather gloves.

'My hands have gone black,' he repeated. 'My hands!'

I realized his mind was wandering, so I just said, 'OK, Vince, put them in your pockets. Get them warm, and the colour will come back to them. Come on now: keep up with me and Stan, mate. Keep going.'

At that point I can't have been thinking straight. What I should have done was to keep hold of him, or actually tie him to me. But that didn't occur to me, and I just kept walking. Stan and I would move on for a bit, then wait for Vince to catch up. Then the same again. I tried to be sharp with him one moment, kind the next. One minute I'd shout, 'Get a grip!' trying to spark him into action. Then I'd become comforting, tap him on the shoulder, and say, 'Come on, Vince, keep walking. Everything will be all right. We're going to get out.'

Vince's behaviour was now swinging wildly. Several times he started yelling out loud – which of course was bad for our nerves, as anybody could have heard him from hundreds of metres off. Stan hissed, 'Vince – be quiet!' and he shut up for a while.

Because hypothermia was setting in, our navigation had become erratic. For some time I'd had the feeling that I was drifting away from reality. The map was saying one thing, and what was happening on the ground seemed to be quite different. We wanted to head north-west, but we kept drifting to the north-east. I saw what was happening, and began to wonder – quite illogically – if I had a tendency to head north-east because I'd been born in the north-east of England. It was just the hypothermia talking.

Every few minutes Stan would say, 'Eh – we're coming off. We're coming off.' Then the clouds would open, and we'd get a glimpse of the Plough, and we could bring ourselves on course again. Then more snow flurries would come in, the stars would be blotted out, and we'd veer off once more.

Struggling as we were, we cracked on for a while –

but then, as we stopped once again, we realized that Vince was no longer with us. When Stan shouted back for him, there was no answer. 'Chris,' he said, 'we've lost him.'

'We can't have,' I answered. 'He must be just behind us.'

We started back on our tracks. Naturally I was worried, but I felt bad-tempered about having to retreat. Where snow was lying, it was easy to follow our footprints; but then there were long stretches of bare rock from which the snow had been blown clear. Whenever we crossed one, we had to cast about on the far side, working forward and back to pick up our trail again. Now we realized how much we'd been zigzagging all over the place.

After twenty minutes there was still no sign of Vince. We called as loud as we dared, and we could see a reasonable distance – but I suddenly realized that our quest was hopeless. It was half an hour, at least, since we'd seen him, and we had no idea what he'd done. He might have walked off to the right; he might have walked off to the left; he might be walking straight backwards; he might have lain down in a hollow and gone to sleep. This last seemed the most likely; that was all he'd been wanting to do for hours. If he had curled up somewhere out of the wind, we could spend all night walking in circles and never find him, probably killing ourselves in the process.

'Stan,' I said, 'I'm making a decision. We're going to turn round and leave him.' I could feel my companion's hesitation, so I added, 'I'll take the responsibility. We've got to leave him, or we'll kill the pair of us.'

'OK, then,' said Stan. 'Fair enough.'

It was a terrible decision to have to take, but I saw no alternative. We had nowhere to take refuge, nowhere to escape from the wind and snow, nowhere to dry our kit and warm up, nowhere to find food. I felt certain that if conditions were the same in the morning, Stan and I would die as well. There was no way we would resuscitate ourselves with no shelter and absolutely nothing to light a fire with.

So with heavy hearts we turned round and cracked on again, and left Vince on his own.

CHAPTER 7
LOOKING BACK

Our only hope was to get down off the high ground into warmer air, and gradually, as we tabbed on, we did seem to be descending. Not steeply, but it felt as if we were losing height. I hoped to God that Vince was doing the same – that he would reach low ground somewhere, get his head down in a hollow, and wake up in the morning.

Our map showed a line of pylons running across our front, and another line that stopped in the middle of nowhere. We thought that if we hit the first set of masts, and then the second, we'd know exactly where we were. But it didn't turn out like that. We only hit the one line of masts, and couldn't find any more. Later we discovered that the second line didn't exist except on the map.

But at least we seemed to be coming down. The snow flurries died out, and the wind became less bitter. Through the night-sight I saw another main road. We approached it, then lay in a hollow to observe it. The hollow turned out to be full of mud: somehow, in the middle of the arid desert, we'd chosen a place like a miniature peat bog.

Ten metres beyond the road we saw a chain-link fence running parallel with it. The fence shone faintly in the moonlight. Beyond it was something pale. It looked like a strip of concrete, and we thought we'd come across some form of installation. It looked like it went on for ever. Then, at the last minute, we realized what it was: a railway line, fenced to keep animals off the track.

The fence was only about two metres high. Any other time, we'd have scaled it in seconds. But we were so cold and helpless we just couldn't climb it. Stan brought out his set of folding Leatherman pliers and, with an all-out effort to make his hands work, cut a vertical slit in the mesh. We knew we were going against the SOP, because anyone who came along and saw the gap would realize that somebody had been through there. But it was the only way we were going to cross the track.

We squeezed through the gap and found ourselves on the railway line. Should we walk along it? It would have been easy going, tabbing on the concrete sleepers. A check on the map showed that it ran straight to a town on the Syrian border. But then we reckoned that the line would probably be patrolled, or that someone on a train would be bound to see us. There was nowhere to hide near the track, and if a train came along, we'd be caught in the open.

We decided to continue northwards. At the fence on the far side of the line Stan gave me the pliers and said, 'Your turn.' My fingers were so numb that I could hardly grip the handles, and putting pressure on them really hurt. But wire by wire I cut a slit, and we wormed through, pulling the chain-link back into place behind us so that the gap wasn't too obvious. With any luck it would be days before anyone noticed the damage.

Leaving the railway, we found a big, rounded hill ahead of us and started up it. A few metres short of the summit we suddenly stopped. In that split second we'd spotted anti-aircraft gun barrels pointing into the sky no more than four or five metres in front of us. Standing still and staring at them, we realized we could see the top of a wall of sandbags, almost under our noses. Obviously there were Iraqis inside the sangar but, thank God, they seemed to be asleep.

Without a word, without turning, we back-tracked down the slope, mere centimetres at a time, watching for any movement to our front. Nothing stirred. Once we were clear, we pulled away eastwards in a big loop, leaving the mound on our left, and then came back onto our northerly heading. But the incident gave us a fright, because we'd been walking carelessly, not worrying about the scrunching noise our boots were making on the loose rock and gravel.

Saturday 26 January: Escape – Day Three

By the early hours of the morning we were back into a system of shallow wadis and dry channels maybe ten metres wide, but less than a metre deep. These river beds were full of little bushes which threw thick, black shadows in the moonlight, so that every hollow seemed to be full of quite dense vegetation. I thought, *Great – we'll be able to get our heads down in here. It should be warmer too.*

About 0530 we started looking for a place to lie up, and settled in a hollow. As I lay down next to Stan, he took off his webbing and laid it down in the middle of some bushes. We cuddled down together on top of it. It was really embarrassing, because we were front to front, with our arms round each other, and we had to take turns on whose head was at the bottom.

So we lay there, shuddering, drifting off into sleep, waking with a start, shaking all over, until dawn broke. By then I was bitterly regretting some of the mistakes I'd made in choosing and packing my kit. Apart from the brew-kit, which would have been a great morale-booster, I should have had a Gore-Tex bivvy bag or at least a space blanket in one of my pouches.

When daylight came, we found that some of the mud had dried on us, helped by our body heat, and our clothes were all stiff and covered with ice crystals, as if they'd been left out on a frosty night. Looking up, I saw that the sky was clear and blue, and thought, *Thank God, it's going to be a fine day*.

Light revealed that the bushes, which had looked promising at night, were nothing but thorny skeletons, eaten down by goats. There wasn't a leaf on them, and they weren't going to hide us from anyone. So we crawled across and tucked ourselves into the wall of a wadi that ran north to south.

At ten o'clock the sun came up and shone on us. I'm sure that saved our lives. One more wet, windy day and we would have drifted off into unconsciousness and never come round. The sun never felt very warm, but it definitely made the air less cold, and we began to sort ourselves out a bit. We took off our webbing, and I spread out my map case to dry. We also cleaned the mud off our weapons and reloaded magazines. I found I'd fired about 70 rounds during the contact. Stan produced a sachet of American corned-beef hash from his belt-kit, and as I watched him eat it, I was thinking, *Why didn't I bring my own rations with me?* All I had was two biscuits, my last.

At one point I said, 'Stan – can you tell me, what are you doing sitting in the middle of Iraq?'

'You know, Chris,' he replied, 'I'm asking myself that, right this very minute.' He burst out laughing. 'I bet we look a total state now.'

'Too right we do.'

'What about *you*, then? What are *you* doing here?'

It was a good question. When I thought about it, I saw that my involvement in the SAS was down to my love of being in open country. It was that, more than anything else, which had made me join the army.

I grew up in Rowlands Gill, a small village in the country just outside Newcastle, and went to the junior school there. From our house, I could walk straight out across the fields and into the forest, and I was always playing in the woods, making camps and sleeping out. My father worked on building sites, but he generally got laid off during the winter. That suited him fine, because all his life he'd been keen on shooting.

Dad would take me shooting in the country around Rowlands Gill. We used to build hides, in which we'd wait for pigeons, or ferret rabbits out of burrows in the hedges. On winter evenings we'd stand in the woods and shoot pigeons as they came into roost.

My dad had a five-shot Browning automatic 12-bore. Once, as we came round a corner, we saw five rabbits on the edge of a field. He got them all, one after another. With feats like that he soon became my hero, and I loved every minute of our expeditions.

But then came a great change. Some time in his thirties, my dad decided it was wrong to shoot birds and animals, and stopped altogether. By then I was mad keen, and kept suggesting we should go out. 'No,' Dad would say, 'you're better off just watching them or taking pictures, capturing them on film. If you want to go, shoot with a camera.'

At an early age I started asking if I could have an air rifle, and my parents kept saying no. At one point my dad bought me a .410, but I was only allowed to take it out with him, under close supervision. Later, when I was thirteen or fourteen, I saved up my pocket money and asked again if I could buy an air rifle. Still the answer was no, so my younger brother Keith and I went out with some older boys and bought one, a BSA .22. I kept the precious weapon hidden in the loft.

Again I asked my mum, 'Can I buy an air rifle?'

'No,' came the reply.

'What if I just get one?'

'You wouldn't be able to keep one in this house without your dad and me knowing.'

Keith and I were looking at each other, thinking, 'Yeah – right!' We used to smuggle the air gun out of the house. Keith would wait on the ground, while I climbed out of my bedroom window and handed the gun down to him. Then we'd run off into the woods and go shooting.

One day, as I came home from school, I found that Keith had got there before me; he grabbed me, his face all fearful. 'Dad's just bought a new TV,' he said, 'and the man's in the loft, putting up the aerial. You'd better get up there quick.'

The hatchway going up into the loft was in my bedroom. I stood there with Keith, waiting anxiously, when my dad called cheerily up to the fitter from downstairs, 'I don't suppose there are any secrets hidden up there?'

Keith and I stared at each other in horror. 'No,' the aerial guy called. 'There's nothing up here.'

The rifle was never discovered – but when I was sixteen or so I owned up, and by then it was too late for anyone to worry.

At school I was quite soft, and used to get bullied. If a girl started making up to me, I'd get beaten up by someone else who fancied her. If there was going to be a fight, it took place when school finished. There'd always be a big crowd gathering at the gate, waiting for the action. Sometimes, if my brother Keith got the worst of an argument, he would say, 'Right – my big brother Chris will see to you.' Then he'd find me at playtime and say, 'By the way, you're to have a fight tonight.' Sometimes I'd go over the back fence and do a runner across the fields to avoid facing the music.

When I was sixteen I decided that this sort of thing had to stop, and I began fighting back. I realized that if you have a fight, you probably get hurt, but it doesn't last for ever. Listening to my dad, and taking a grip of myself, I put a stop to the bullying.

I also started judo lessons, and couldn't get enough of them. At first, for a couple of months, I was taught by a Japanese man who practised a pure form of the ancient martial art. Then I moved to an instructor in Newcastle, an ex-Olympic champion, who taught me to fight dirty. I became so keen that I'd go into town almost every night, and I started winning competitions. But I gave up judo when, in a fight with a bigger boy, my clavicle became detached from my rib cage. Although I finished the fight, I lost on points – and afterwards the injury caused me so many problems that I thought I'd better stop. But I found judo good for getting rid of aggression.

As I lay there in the Iraqi desert, I remembered the sick fear I once felt when I was a kid of about thirteen. We were playing Knocking Nine Doors, and a big guy rushed out and chased us down the street. He was known as a really hard man, and when we belted on his door, he was waiting behind it. He flew out, and we went hurtling down the road. He chased us for a couple of hours, and the terror I'd felt then was exactly the same as that I experienced during the contact in the wadi.

That wasn't the only time I'd been on the run. Once, Keith and I had been playing football with some other boys. I must have hurt one of them in a tackle, and he went off in a rage. Later, Keith and I set out with our cousin to get conkers. I'd just climbed the tree and started hitting the conkers down, when Keith gave a hoarse cry: 'Chris, look!' Peering down through the leaves, I saw a gang of ten or twelve kids from the village, all armed with sticks, heading for us at a run.

'There they are!' the raiders shouted as they spotted us. 'There they are!'

I jumped down from the tree. 'You run back up home that way,' I told Keith, and I took off in the other direction. The pack came after me – and it was like hare and hounds for the rest of the day, four hours at least. I ran until I thought I was going to die. I ran through the forest, waded the river, ran up onto the moors – and still they were after me. In the end I spotted a neighbour of my aunt's, a man who worked as a gamekeeper. I came tearing down the road with the hunters close behind and threw myself into his arms, unable to speak.

I hated school work. I was all right at maths and technical drawing, but never much good at basics like reading and writing, and I took little interest in most of my lessons. Afterwards, I bitterly regretted not trying harder at school, especially when I found, as an adult, that I had a perfectly good brain. As a boy, though, I was more interested in making a camp in the woods or racing about with the other kids on the estate than in going to school.

By the time I was sixteen, all I wanted was to join the army. At the local recruiting office I did the first tests to become a boy soldier, and passed them fine. For the final tests I was due to travel to Sutton Coldfield, but I went down with jaundice and missed the interviews. I was really upset, but I remember lying in bed, feeling lousy, and seeing two men in uniform come to the house. They told my parents I should join up as a man when I was seventeen or eighteen.

Luckily for me, my cousin Billy was in 23 SAS, the Territorials unit made up of part-time volunteers. One day he said, 'Why not come up, and we'll get you out on a couple of weekends? Then you'll see what it's like to be in the army.'

So I went up to Prudhoe, in Northumberland, where 'C' Squadron of 23 SAS had its base. At that time – the late 1970s, before the famous siege of the Iranian Embassy – the SAS was nothing like as well known as it later became. I was just a naive lad of sixteen, and as I walked through the doors of the drill hall, I saw all these guys who looked really old. No doubt I looked a bit of a twerp to them. But nothing could damp down my excitement; when the SQMS took me into the stores and gave me a camouflage suit, a set of webbing pouches, a poncho and a bergen, I was over the moon.

A bunch of recruits had assembled for a weekend's training – some were civilians, others from regular army units. Their average age must have been about twenty-five. As I arrived, they were about to have a map-reading lesson, so I sat down with them and did that. Next, we all scrambled onto trucks and drove up to Otterburn, where we walked out onto the moors. 'Right,' somebody said. 'Tonight we're going to sleep against this wall, under ponchos.'

I thought it was terrific – to spend the night outdoors. I was so excited that I couldn't go to sleep, and I lay for ages gazing up at the stars.

Next morning, after no more than a couple of hours' sleep, I was up early, and we spent the day walking. We'd walk for a while, have something to eat, get another lesson in map-reading, then go on again. The exercise ended with a long hike, which left me exhausted.

Back at Prudhoe, I thought, *Well – that was great. But that's it.* I imagined that after my introduction to the army, I wouldn't be asked again. But luckily for me the OC happened to be there. He was a scary-looking guy, with ginger hair and little glasses, and looked a right hard nut. He came over to speak to me and said, 'You're Billy's cousin, aren't you? Would you like to come back up?'

'Fine,' I said. 'Great.'

'Good,' he replied. 'But you must understand that you won't be on the books. You shouldn't be here, really, because we're breaking the law. If anything happens, you won't be able to blame the army.'

That didn't worry me one bit, and from then on I went up to Prudhoe every weekend.

The selection course took place over a period of three months, with the recruits assembling only at weekends. At first the group had consisted of sixty people, and every week a few of them decided they'd had enough and gave up. But for me things became more and more exciting, because we went from being in a big group to working in pairs, and in the end I was on my own. It was a big thrill when someone told me to walk alone from Point A to Point B. I had become confident with my map-reading, and between Friday night and Sunday morning we'd cover up to sixty kilometres, carrying a bergen. On the last weekend of the course, there were only four of us left, and I was the only one who finished the march.

Normally, anyone who finished that march would be tested for two weeks on the Brecon Beacons. But I was too young to go, and they told me that I wouldn't be ready to take selection for 23 SAS until two more Territorials selection courses had gone through. In other words, I was going to have to wait a whole year.

That was disappointing, but I was so keen that I volunteered to keep going on the Territorials weekends when the next course started. By that time I knew all the routes, and I could run from one checkpoint to another without a map. I'd also learned how to cut corners and cheat a bit. At the end of that course only one man passed: he and I were the sole survivors.

By then I'd become a bit of a joke in the squadron, but on the third course I was so fit, and knew the ground so well, that I finished each leg before the other guys were halfway.

Now at last I was old enough to go down to Wales for the Test Week. After two weeks on the hills, based at Sennybridge, I passed out and at last became a member of 'C' Squadron.

I was a member of the SAS!

My aim, of course, was to join 22, the regular

SAS. Normally, to do that, you have to enrol in another regiment first, as the regular SAS is a specialized regiment within the British army. My best course seemed to be to join the Parachute Regiment, but all the guys said, 'Don't bother with that. Once you've served here in 23 for a bit, you can go straight on to selection for 22.' Apart from that, 22 were holding a lot of courses and exercises down at Hereford, and there were often spare places – so I was going south a good deal.

By this time I was extremely fit. Every day I'd do a six-kilometre run, followed by a ten-kilometre bike ride, and then swim two kilometres, and run the four kilometres home.

At last – at the age of twenty-two, over six years since I had first started going to 23 TA – the time came for me to go down to Hereford and take the 22 selection course. This was spread over six months in total.

We began with four weeks on the hills, then two weeks' tactics training, followed by five weeks in the jungle in Brunei, then combat survival followed by continuation training.

In the hills there were some days when I felt we

were being crucified, but on the whole it wasn't too bad.

In tactics training, I found I was confident with a weapon, but I was shocked by the state of some of the troops who came up: their weapon-handling drills were poor, to say the least.

In the jungle we were put into six-man patrols, and sent to live in a base camp from which we moved out every day to do range work, navigation or RV drills. I found it tough-going. Navigation posed no problem, and I discovered that I could mix with other guys easily enough. But I didn't like the physical difficulties of living in the jungle, where you're wet, filthy and stinking for weeks on end.

Back at Hereford, at the end of the course, we were all taken into the camp cinema. Nothing had been said about who had passed or failed. Then the sergeant major announced that he would read out a list of names. The people on it were to go back to the accommodation block, wait there, and return in fifteen minutes' time. He read out twenty names, including mine. Had we passed or failed? Nobody knew. Returning to the cinema a quarter of an hour later, we found that the other half of the course had disappeared. We sat down again. The sergeant major stood up and said, 'Right, you lot. You haven't passed . . .'

There was an intake of breath. Everyone's heart hit the floor.

'. . . *yet*,' he added.

Faces lit up. Everyone burst out laughing. There was more training to come – but so what?

We did combat survival – in which six more of the guys failed – and after that, build-up for Northern Ireland and the counter-terrorist team. Then, at last, the survivors passed, and we were given our berets. It was a tremendous thrill for me. After my years in the Territorials, I'd finally achieved my goal.

Now, at the age of twenty-three, I was a member of 22 SAS!

Each member of the SAS is also attached to a regular army unit, which is known as their 'parent unit'. If Special Forces work doesn't work out for any reason, the serving soldier can then be RTU'd – returned to unit – so they are no longer in the SAS, but are still in the British army. Most recruits come to selection from their units, but as I'd gone straight from the Territorials, I had to have a parent unit now I was in the Regiment. I chose the Parachute

Regiment, and spent eight weeks with them before returning to Hereford.

As soon as I became a member of 'B' Squadron I did a couple of exercises with Government agents in the United Kingdom and Europe. In one, which was highly realistic, we flew into Jersey in the middle of the night, our helicopter landing in a public park, to kidnap a businessman who – according to the scenario – had been in touch with the Soviets and might defect. Wearing civilian clothes, we booked into hotels and made contact with agents who already had the target under surveillance. Then, having hired a van, we snatched him as he came out of a restaurant late at night. After a quick transfer to a car, we drove to a pick-up point on the coast and the helicopter, which had been cruising out of sight off-shore, slipped in at wave-top height to land on the beach and collect us.

That was the first time I'd been exposed to anything of the kind, and I thought, *This is for me!*

Next I went on to the SP (Special Projects) or anti-terrorist team, and found it really exciting. Part of the team was on stand-by the whole time, for immediate response to a threat like the hijacking of an aircraft. We all trained to a very high level, each guy putting down at least a thousand rounds a week.

I loved being in the SAS, and was fiercely loyal to it. But as I lay against the bank of the wadi, Hereford seemed a long way off. I knew I would have to rely on every second of my training if I was going to get out of the Iraqi desert alive . . .

CHAPTER 8
DOWN TO ONE

We'd become so confused during the night that it took us some time to work out which day this was. We decided it was Saturday morning. Time passed slowly, but we weren't too uncomfortable. The sun was reviving us, we were chatting in low voices, and we thought the River Euphrates was only just over the next hill to the north, which was cheering.

We said to ourselves, 'We'll hit the river, get some water, and walk out into Syria – no problem.' We told ourselves we were safe for the time being, and that one more good night's push would bring us to the Syrian border. We'd put so much ground between us and the scene of the contact that we didn't think anyone would come looking for us.

Of course, we were wondering about Vince.

I hoped against hope that, like us, he'd found a warmer place; but in my heart of hearts I felt that he was dead. I imagined him lying down in a hole among the snow, falling asleep, and drifting away, without any pain or knowledge of what was happening. At the back of my mind I also kept hoping that we would see the rest of the patrol appear – that we'd hear one of them say something and they'd pop up out of the ground.

I took off my boots – one at a time, in case we were surprised – to have a look at my feet. As I thought, they were badly blistered along the sides, especially round the ball, and on the heels. But I had nothing to treat them with, and could only put my boots back on again.

We spent an hour cleaning our weapons, which were covered in mud and grit, doing them one at a time in case we got bounced. In my right-hand pouch I had a small but well-stocked kit – pull-through, four-by-two-inch cleaning patches, oil, rag, and a tool like a pocket knife fitted with a screwdriver, scraper and gouge. With this I gave my 203 a thorough going-over. I pulled a piece of four-by-two through the barrel, cleaned and oiled the working parts, and checked the loaded magazines to make sure no grit had got in among the rounds. By working carefully, I stripped the weapon and reassembled it making hardly a sound. If you release the working parts of a 203 normally, they snap forward with a sharp crack, but if you handle them gently, you don't need to make a sound.

Then, at about midday, we heard the noise we'd already learned to dread: the jingle of bells.

Goats! Again!

We went down flat with our weapons and looked along the little valley. There they were – a scatter of brown, black, grey and dirty white animals, coming slowly into the wadi from the north-east. Then their minder appeared and sat down on a rock in full view, only fifty metres away. He was a young man with thick, curly black hair and stubbled cheeks. There he sat, daydreaming, kicking his feet, chewing on stalks of dead grass.

The goats began feeding our way. Stan and I lay still with our 203s ready. 'Right,' I whispered. 'If he comes up on us, we're going to have to take him out.'

I didn't want to kill a civilian. But I felt certain that if the man saw us, he'd go back to the nearest habitation and give us away. It flashed through

118

my mind that we could tie him up. But if we did that, he might die of exposure. I thought, *He's either going to escape or die – so we might as well do him now.*

The goats kept feeding and moving towards us. They reached our position. When they saw us, they jerked their heads up, but that was all – a jerk, and on they'd go. All this while the herder was sitting there, looking up at the sky now and then. Certainly he hadn't locked on to anything.

'He's bound to come after them,' I breathed, 'and if he does, we'll do him.'

We didn't want to fire a shot, for obvious reasons, but both of us had knives. Mine was a folding knife – a good one, but with a small blade. Stan had a k-bar bayonet on his webbing with a six- or seven-inch blade.

But Stan, being a gentleman and a good soldier, wasn't happy. 'Shouldn't we take the chance of seeing if he's got a vehicle? We could nick it and drive off.'

'No, we'll do him.'

The young man stood up.

He looked quite a big guy – about the size of Stan, and hefty with it. Immediately I changed my plan.

'Stan,' I whispered, 'give us that knife. You grab him and I'll do him.'

'No,' Stan muttered. 'You're not having it.'

'Then *you'd* better do him . . .'

Suddenly it was too late. With the guy nearly on top of us, Stan jumped up and grabbed him.

'Sit down, mate!' he said loudly. 'How're you doing? Good? Right! Sit down!'

The guy jumped, and let out a stream of Arabic, but Stan forced him down on the bank-side. I sat down too, staring at him. He was in his twenties and dressed like the village idiot in a big old overcoat of what looked like dark grey tweed. His hair was messy and he had several ragged jumpers on under the overcoat and slip-on leather shoes. He kept looking at me, but I didn't say anything.

Stan did all the talking. 'Car?' he asked. 'Tractor?' He made driving motions with his hands. 'House?'

He drew in the air, but our visitor didn't understand a word of English. All he said was '*Aiwa*', which means 'Yes'.

'Where's there a vehicle?'

'*Aiwa.*'

'How far to walk?'

'*Aiwa.*'

'Listen,' Stan said after a bit. 'I'll go with him and see if we can get a tractor.'

It seemed incredible to me that Stan should want to go off with a total stranger. I reminded him that we were aliens in a foreign country, where we had no business to be. I knew we'd get no friendly help from the Iraqis. 'Suppose this was World War Two,' I said, 'and we were a couple of German paratroopers, lost in the Welsh mountains. We meet this farm lad and try to chat him up. Of course he'd say he's going to help us. But what does he want really? To get us in the nick. Nothing else.'

Even that didn't change Stan's mind. 'It's OK,' he said. 'I'll take the risk and go with him.'

'No, Stan. You're staying here.'

'Chris, I want to go.'

I thought he was crazy. But I couldn't force him to stay. 'OK,' I told him. 'I can't order you, because we're on our own. But listen, mate: I don't want you to go. It'll mean us splitting up. You'll be on your own. You're making a big mistake here.'

'No, no,' he said. 'I'll leave my weapon and webbing with you. Then I won't look so aggressive. I'll just walk next to him.'

I could see he was determined. 'All right,' I told

him, 'I'll wait here for you till six-thirty, last light. If you're not back by then, I'm off on this bearing.' And I gave him the northerly course we'd already decided on.

'Fair enough,' he said.

'Go on, then. When you're out of sight, I'll take your weapon and webbing fifty metres up that dry stream bed, and hide them there.'

So Stan stood up with the Arab and said, 'Come on, cobber. Let's go.' The two of them started walking off, with the Arab whistling for his goats to follow. I crawled down to the bottom of the wadi where I sat and watched them. When they'd gone a couple of hundred metres, I suddenly thought, *No! This is wrong!* and I yelled out, '*Stan!* Stan, come back here!'

Back he came, almost running.

'Think about what you're doing,' I told him. 'Leave your webbing if you like, but at least take your weapon.'

'I don't want to look too aggressive.'

'Sling it over your shoulder then, and carry it down the side of your body – but have it with you. And if you change your mind, put one into him and we'll sit the day out together.'

But Stan was overboard about his new friend. 'No, no, Chris,' he said. 'He's all right. He's offered me food.'

'What food?'

'It's only a few berries, but I trust the guy. He seems friendly. If we get to a vehicle, I'll give him a sovereign.'

Away Stan went with the Iraqi, meandering down the dry stream bed. For nearly a kilometre he remained in sight. He'd wrapped his shamag round his head, and from a distance he looked quite like another Arab. I could see the two of them trying to chat together, matey as anything. In the end they went round a bend to the left and disappeared.

Now I'm on my own, I thought.

Time crawled by. After a couple of hours I took Stan's webbing and tucked it into the side of the stream bed, where I'd told him it would be. On top of it I left four of the extra 203 rounds which I'd taken from Vince. Then I had nothing to do but wait for dark.

As the hours dragged past, I grew more and more jumpy. Several times I imagined I heard something. Whenever that happened, I'd look out, hoping to see Stan returning.

Dusk came on. By 1730 I was very anxious. I'd have to make a decision soon. I was hungry, thirsty, cold and on my own. Six o'clock came. I took one last look back down the wadi. Night had come down, and there was still no sign. I kept hoping I'd see the lights of a vehicle heading out – but there was nothing.

It was a tough decision. My last friend had disappeared. He could still be on his way back. But when 1830 came, I thought, *This is it. You can't sit around here any longer.*

So I checked my compass and started walking north.

Alone.

Saturday 26 January: Escape – Night Three
For fifteen minutes I tabbed it steadily over level, open ground, with darkness settling in on the desert all round me. Then I happened to look over my shoulder, and I saw a set of headlights coming up the wadi I'd just left. *Stan's got a vehicle after all,* I thought. *Brilliant!*

I started running back as fast as I could. I must have been halfway back to my start-point when suddenly I saw that it wasn't one set of lights coming towards me, but two. Immediately I thought, *He can't have two vehicles. He must have been captured, and this is the enemy. If he'd been on his own, he'd never have brought two vehicles.* So I turned and ran north again.

Already I was out of breath. Behind me, the vehicles had driven up the side of the wadi and were heading straight across the open desert towards me. The clouds parted and the moon shone through, lighting the place up like day. It may have been my imagination, but my smock seemed to have become luminous, shining like an electric beacon. The old adrenalin had started up, and my heart was going like a sledgehammer. Then I saw a little bush with a shadow behind it, and threw myself down into that tiny patch of black.

As I lay there panting, I frantically sorted out my kit. I checked the magazine on the 203, and piled spare mags in a heap beside me. I opened out the 66 so that it was ready to fire. I even bent together the ends of the safety pins on my white phos grenades, so that I could whip them out quickly if need be.

For a moment I got a breather. The lights swung round, whipping wildly up and down as the vehicles went over bumps and headed back into the wadi. I heard the banging of doors. Obviously some guys had got out to have a look round the place where the goatherd had found us in the morning. I squinted through the night-sight, trying to make out what they were doing, but the glare from the lights shone everything else out. Then the vehicles moved off again and started driving about the floor of the wadi.

The moment the lights were away from me, I picked up my kit, stuffed things into the webbing pouches down my front, and legged it.

Now I was *really* running, looking right and left for cover. Suddenly the lights swung round again and they were coming at me. I dropped down and got my kit out once more. I set up the 203 with the battle-sight, and as I piled the spare magazines, it went through my mind that this was just like range practice. I cocked the 66 again, lifted the bomb-sights on the 203, and waited.

I didn't know if they'd seen me or not. But they were driving towards me at a steady roll. I got the 66 lined up on the leading pair of lights and listened to the sound of my heart pounding.

The lights were still coming. Obviously the

vehicles weren't going to stop. Someone on board must have realized that I would be heading due north, going for the river, and they were driving on that bearing. The wagons were rolling at maybe 15 mph, and the lights were quite steady. They would pass so close that there was no chance of them not seeing me.

It was them or me.

I hugged the ground and tried to stop myself shaking. An age seemed to pass as the vehicles ground on.

Fifty metres, and they kept coming.

There were two Land Rover-type vehicles. I couldn't tell how many men they might contain. As they approached, I held the sight of the 66 aligned between the front pair of lights. When they were twenty metres off, I pulled the trigger.

Whooooosh! went the launcher, right in my ear. Out front there was a big *bang* as the rocket took the vehicle head-on. There was no flash. Just a heavy explosion, and a cloud of white smoke billowing out in the moonlight.

The vehicle rolled to a stop.

I dropped the 66, grabbed the 203 and lined up the grenade-sight on the second pair of lights, a few metres to the left of the first. From maybe forty metres I smacked that one right in the bonnet.

Then I was up and running towards the enemy.

In a moment I had reached the first vehicle and put a burst into it. Coming to the second, I sprayed it all down the side, through the canvas back. Then I looked into the back and put another burst in. There were men in the back wearing dishdashes. I let off another burst into the driver's compartment. Then I had to change magazines. At the front again, I put more rounds into the first vehicle. Both vehicles were now in bits.

Only then did I realize I'd left the other magazines piled up at my firing point. I sprinted back to them, snatched them up, stuffed them down the front of my smock and ran.

I ran till I thought my heart was going to burst. I imagined that everybody was on to me and chasing me. The moon was so bright that I felt as if a spotlight was beaming down on me. I was swept up in panic, just as I had been when chased as a kid. It was as if I'd been found out, and was on my own. I ran till I *had* to slow down: my throat was heaving, my chest exploding, my mouth dry as the desert.

I'd had no water all through that day, and soon I was so tired that it was painful even to walk.

All the time I was turning to look behind, to see if any more lights were coming up – but nothing showed. At last I thought it was safe to stop, sit down and sort out my equipment.

After a contact like that, it takes time to recover. Gradually I chilled out and got myself together. One minor improvement was that I had less to carry: once I'd fired the 66 I threw away the tube, which was useless to the Iraqis.

Walking again, I kept on for a couple of hours towards the north. All the time I was wondering what had happened to Stan, and hoping he hadn't come back in one of the vehicles. Or had he sent them up to me? No, I decided: he couldn't have. It must have been the goatherd who brought the Iraqis back to the wadi; no one else could have directed them onto my position with such accuracy. My intuition about him had been right. I should never have let Stan go off with him.

The question was, what had happened back on the site of the contact while I had been heading north? If anyone had got away from one of the vehicles I'd hit, or if someone else had found the wrecks, word might have gone out that another enemy soldier was on the run. People would surely guess that I was heading for the Euphrates. From the firepower I'd put down, they might even have thought that there were several of us.

I tabbed on and on through the moonlight. Now the desert was rolling in gentle undulations, and I believed that the river was going to appear over every rise. Then, to my right, I heard dogs barking, kids shouting, grown-ups calling. As I went down on one knee to listen, I saw the red tracer of anti-aircraft fire going up in the distance. Obviously there were habitations somewhere close to me, and the people I could hear were watching that nice firework display on the horizon. Then I heard the far-off roar of jets. They must have been miles off, attacking some target, and the red tracer was curving silently up towards the stars.

Half an hour later I spotted a glimmer of light ahead. The night-sight picked out three stationary vehicles, with light coming out of the side. I went down and watched for signs of people on foot, in case a mobile patrol was being deployed to cut me off. Men on foot could be strung out in an extended line, sweeping the desert ahead of them. But I saw nothing more, so I avoided the vehicles and carried on.

Again, as I came to the top of a rise, I was convinced that I must find the Euphrates in front of me – but no. The next thing I saw was a set of pylons. I'd been expecting them for some time, because they were marked on my map. Beyond them was a main supply route, and some fifteen kilometres beyond that, the river. When I sat down under the power lines and scanned ahead, I found I could see the road, and a wide-open flat area beyond it – but no water.

I knew that in Biblical times the Euphrates had been a mighty waterway, and I assumed that it must still be pretty big. But after I crossed the main supply route, all I hit was a huge system of dry wadis, with steep walls up to twenty metres high. Obviously they'd once been a river bed. Maybe in wet weather flash floods would turn the channels into a rushing river again. I was gagging for want of water, and getting so confused in my mind that suddenly I thought, *I hope this isn't the Euphrates. Surely it can't have dried out since the Bible? If it has, I'm finished.*

Panic was making me walk faster and scrabble down through the tumbled, loose rock. I kept thinking, *There's got to be water at the bottom of this.* At its lowest point the river bed seemed to open out, and as I looked down through the night-sight, I made out a line of palm trees running across my front from left to right. Also, away to my right, I could see the houses of a village. I still couldn't see any water, but I thought, *This has got to be the river – the Euphrates, at last.* I started walking down towards the trees, which I presumed were growing on the bank.

The closer I came, the warmer the air seemed to be – or at least, the atmosphere seemed stiller and calmer. I kept about 300 metres from the edge of the village, but dogs came out and started barking. As there was no wind, they could hardly have smelled me. They'd probably picked up the noise of my feet. The houses were dark. They may have been blacked out on purpose, but more likely the people in them were asleep.

Moving along to the boundary wall of the village, I made my way carefully down to the river through oblong fields. No crops were sprouting as yet, but the ground had been well tilled, and the fields were divided up by irrigation ditches, with grass growing here and there. I tried to keep out of the fields, in case I left footprints in the soft soil. Instead, I kept to the ditches, which as yet had no water in them.

At last, between the trunks of the palm trees, I saw water. Irrigation pumps were working all along the bank: the night was full of their quick, steady beat – *boop*, *boop*, *boop*, *boop*. I could hear many different pumps working up and down the valley. For several minutes I kept still, watching for any movement. The cultivation seemed to end about ten metres from the edge of the water, and my night-sight revealed piles of cut bushes, each about two metres square, sticking out from the bank into the stream, one about every fifty metres. At first I couldn't make out what they were for, then it occurred to me that they were probably makeshift jetties, for men to fish off or to bring boats alongside. Using one for cover, I crept right down to the water's edge.

Crouching next to the pile, I got out my water bottles, but found that at the bank the water was only a few millimetres deep – a thin skin over mud. I tried to wade out, but I hadn't taken three steps before my feet plunged deep into silt. In a second I was up to my knees, then up to my waist. I was sinking. I threw my rifle back onto the pile of bushes and dragged myself out, soaked up to the waist and coated in slimy, silty mud.

For my next attempt, I crawled out over one of the platforms of bushes. As my weight came onto it, the whole structure sank into the stream. I could feel water coming through my clothes at the front, but I filled both bottles, crawled back out, and drank one down.

I swallowed and gasped and choked, trying to stifle the noise. The relief of getting water down my neck was incredible. I shone my torch beam down the neck of the full bottle, and saw that the water was black and foul-looking, but it tasted quite good. I crawled out to fill the empty bottle again.

At that point the river was a couple of hundred metres wide, and I could see no buildings or cultivations on the far bank. In the moonlight the land beyond glowed white, as if it were covered in salt. I thought about swimming across, because it would be safer on the far side. But although I'm a strong swimmer, I realized that to go in with my weapon and webbing would be asking for trouble. The water was icy cold, and although the surface was smooth, I could see that a strong current was flowing out in the middle of the stream. If I'd got into difficulties halfway across, that would have been it.

By then it was nearly five o'clock in the morning. I needed somewhere to lie up for the day.

I moved cautiously out between scattered houses, up to a dirt road. Again a dog started barking, so I waited a couple of minutes before going on up into the dry wadi systems. Once into the rocks I turned on my TACBE and tried speaking into it. There was no response, so I left the beacon on for a while. As I climbed, the rocky channels grew steeper and steeper. A couple of hundred metres above the road, they came to a dead end. There I found a rock a metre or so high which was casting a black shadow in the moonlight. I curled up beside it, with my map case beneath my legs, one shamag round them and the other round my head. I lay there feeling fairly safe in that patch of deep darkness.

Before settling down, I gave myself the only treat at my disposal: I got out my flask, and took a nip of whisky. The spirit burned as it went down into my empty stomach, but it gave me a momentary lift.

I was so exhausted that in spite of the cold I kept falling asleep, only to come round with a start a few minutes later, racked by shudders. It was a real pain to be wet again; having spent hours with Stan getting dry, I was now soaked all up the front, with my sodden clothes clinging to me, and the damp making the cold even worse.

When first light came, with dawn breaking early under clear skies, I realized that I wasn't really in any sort of cover. At night the shadow of the rock had looked comforting; if someone had walked past in the dark, he wouldn't have seen me. Now I found I was lying out in the open.

Looking up onto the north bank of the wadi, I saw a hollow among some loose rocks. I walked up to it, lay inside, and piled up a few more rocks at either side to break up the outline of my body. That was the best place I could find in which to spend the day.

And it was only then that it really hit me how much I was on my own.

CHAPTER 9
BOXING CLEVER

Sunday 27 January: Escape – Day Four

In the days and nights that followed, there were several moments when my morale plunged to rock-bottom. This was one of them. A wave of loneliness swept over me as I realized that I was utterly alone. I was hungry, wet, tired, cut off from all communication with friends, and still far inside a hostile country. I thought it couldn't get any worse.

'If things get on top of you,' my mum always used to say, 'have a good cry.' So I lay there in the rocks and tried to cry – but I couldn't. Instead my face crumpled up and I started laughing. Somehow it did the trick. It got rid of the tension and sorted me out. I daydreamed about the glorious puddings my mum used to make – particularly her rice pudding, with its thick, sweet, creamy inside and its crust baked to a crisp golden brown. I could have done with a helping of that, there and then. But from that point on I wasn't bothered about being alone. All I had to do was get on with heading for the border.

It was the morning of Sunday 27 January, and I'd been on the run for three nights. I would have liked to let my feet breathe, but that would have involved too great a risk. I had to be ready to leg it at any minute: so it was one boot off, one sock off, check that foot, and get sock and boot back on. Then the other foot. The blisters looked bad. They had burst, and the skin below was raw and bleeding. My toenails had started lifting, and there were blisters under my toes. I had no way of treating them, and could only hope that my feet would hold out until I reached the border.

With my boots back on, I spent an hour cleaning my weapon again. I took care, as before, not to make any noise that would carry. Once I had everything squared away, I lay back with my belt undone but my webbing still in place, straps over my shoulders, so that I could make a quick getaway if need be.

Even down there, almost on the level of the

Euphrates, the air was still icy cold, and I was shivering. I lay on one side, with my hands between my legs, tucked in under one big rock. Smaller rocks pulled into position shielded my head and feet, and there was bare rock beneath me.

From time to time I dozed off, but always I woke with a start a few minutes later, shaking all over. It was my body's defence to bring me round like that: if I hadn't kept waking, I would have drifted off and been gone for ever. Aching from contact with the rock, I would shift about, trying to find a more comfortable position. There was always a pebble or bump of rock digging into some part of me, and the pressure points on the outsides of my knees, hips and spine had already begun to rub sore.

The water had made me feel better in one way; but it had given me the shivers, and all I wanted to do was press on again, so that I could warm up. The hardest thing was to keep still in daylight. The urge to start walking, to make progress towards the border, was almost overwhelming.

Below me, the wadi dropped towards the river in a V-shape, snaking left and right. There was nothing alive to keep me interested: no bird or animal, nothing moving. Boredom soon became another powerful enemy. It took all my willpower to resist the urge to move on, or even just to have a look around.

The day was quiet: I never heard voices or traffic movement. Now and then the wind would stir among the rocks and I would come fully alert, looking round, wondering if a person or an animal had shifted. From where I lay I could see what looked like the remains of an ancient viaduct, jutting out from the bank of the river into the water. I wondered how old it was, and whether it could date back as far as the Romans. Round the base of the arches the water was obviously deep, because through my binoculars I could see the current swirling fast. The river was brown with silt, a strong contrast with the salty-looking land on the far bank.

What kept my spirits up was the thought that I must be close to the Syrian border – no more than thirty or forty kilometres away. Looking at the map again and again, I worked out that I was much farther west than I had thought I was. I reckoned I was within one night's march, possibly two, of safety.

Until then, the longest I'd ever gone without food was four days, on combat survival training in Wales.

Even then, an agent had brought me one slice of bread or a little piece of cheese every twenty-four hours – but I remembered feeling pretty weak at the end. The furthest I'd ever walked in one march was sixty-five kilometres – the final march on Selection. Now, I reckoned, I'd covered about 150 kilometres in three nights, and already it was five days since I'd had a proper meal – the big blow-out at Al Jouf. With my biscuits finished, I began to worry about how long my strength would hold out. How long could I go on walking? Would I slow right down, or even be unable to keep going at all?

I knew from weight-training, and books about the subject, that when the body is under stress it starts to burn its own muscle, trying to preserve fat for emergencies. I was carrying very little fat anyway, so I knew my muscles would waste away quite quickly, especially as I was burning yet more energy by shivering all the time. In lectures on combat survival, we'd been told that a man lost in the desert can only survive for a day without water – but this wasn't a typical desert, because the temperature was so low.

I kept wondering about the rest of the patrol. I greatly feared that Vince was dead, and in a way

I felt responsible. Lying all day by the tank berm had definitely contributed to his collapse, and it was me who had said we should follow SOPs and stay there. Then, in the night, I should have tied him to me. As a qualified mountain guide, I could have handled the situation better. But at the time I'd been going down with exposure myself, and not thinking as clearly as I might have.

What about Stan? It seemed certain that he'd been captured, and I could only hope he wasn't having too bad a time. As for the other five . . . I reckoned that a chopper must have come back and lifted them out. I felt sure that the aircraft must have been inbound towards our original position, following the normal Lost Comms procedure, and that it would have flown around until the guys made contact with the pilot. In fact, as I found out later, the other guys in the patrol had been captured that day close to the river at a point about a hundred kilometres nearer to the Syrian border. As a result of contacts with them, 1,600 Iraqi troops had been deployed to look for other Coalition soldiers on the run, and the civilian population along the river had been alerted.

* * *

Sunday 27 January: Escape – Night Four

I came out of my hiding place not long after dark, and began heading north-west, keeping as close as I could to the edge of the cultivated land, where the going was easiest.

I was walking more carefully now, because I was in a populated area. I was probably down to three or four kilometres an hour. Occasionally, for a change, I rested the 203 over my shoulder, but for most of the time I held it in both hands, with the weight taken by the sling of paracord round my neck. That way, the weapon was less tiring on my arms, but it was also at the ready: I could have aimed and fired a shot within a second.

Soon I found that there were amazing numbers of Arabs out and about. Every half hour or so I'd come across a group standing or sitting around, chatting in quiet voices. Several times I picked up the glow of a cigarette and had to box round it. (Boxing is when you walk in a box shape round an obstacle, counting your paces and turning right-angles so you end up walking in the same direction as before.) Often I just smelled smoke, either from cigarettes or from a fire or stove, and pulled off without seeing anything. It seemed odd that so many citizens should be out of doors on a freezing winter night.

Again and again I saw or sensed people ahead of me, brought up the night-sight for a better look, and had to make a detour. In the end my lack of progress became quite frustrating, and I started to think that if things were going to be like this all the way to the border, I would never get out. I would become too weak from lack of food, and would end up getting captured.

During that night I was on the move for eight hours, and must have covered thirty or forty kilometres, but I made only about ten kilometres towards the frontier. I would walk gently forward for a while, see someone, back off and box them. Immediately I'd come on someone else, box them, and carry on. It was zigzag, zigzag, all the time, five or ten steps sideways for every one forward.

I found it incredibly difficult to maintain concentration for any length of time. Wild animals like antelopes and deer, which are preyed on by carnivores, have the ability to remain on the alert for hours on end. Their lives depend on it. But humans have lost the knack, and it takes conscious effort to stay watchful.

Often I found I was having silent conversations with myself.

I'll walk as far as the top of that hill, I'd say. *Then I can have a rest.*

Soon I'd ask, *How did you get yourself into this mess? And where have the others got to now?* Casting ahead in my mind, I wondered what the border with Syria would look like, and how I'd cross it. People and personalities from my past kept drifting into my head: my mum and dad, my brothers, my school teachers. I'd wonder what they'd be doing at that moment – and I longed to tell them where I was. I imagined how surprised they'd be if they knew what I was doing. Often I heard their voices, and these became so real that I'd forget about my own security and pay no attention to my surroundings. Suddenly I'd come to and realize that I'd covered a kilometre or more in a dream.

Whenever I passed a house, the dogs would start barking, and the noise would ricochet down the valley. One lot of dogs would alert the next, and they'd start up before I even reached them. Those tell-tale alarm calls progressed along the river ahead of me, and to my ears they sounded as loud as the wail of a siren.

The dogs were a real nuisance. As I was skirting one village, above me on a mound, I looked up at the houses – square, dark silhouettes with flat roofs and no lights showing – and saw a whole pack of them coming down, barking their heads off. Through the night-sight I watched them make straight for me. One ran up to within three metres, with four or five more close behind it. If I stopped, they would stop, and also they'd stop barking. But the moment I threatened them or moved, they'd bark like hell again and creep on some more, stalking me.

I kept looking anxiously up at the houses, expecting lights to come on at any second. I felt like the Pied Piper, with all the dogs following me. I stopped, picked up a rock and hurled it. The pack ran away for a few metres, only to close in again. As I cleared the houses, they followed for a couple of hundred metres. They stopped, and stood or sat, watching and barking until I was out of their sight. Then, when my nerves were in tatters, they turned back and trooped home. The one saving grace was that their owners seemed to pay no attention whatsoever. So far as I could see, nobody ever came out of a house to see what the noise was all about.

For a while I stayed as close to the river as I could,

partly for navigation, partly so that I could get more water when I needed it. But then, deciding I was too close to the inhabited stretch, I drew away to the south again and returned to the edge of the desert. There I started cross-graining through the wadis, which were running down towards the Euphrates at right-angles to the way I was going. I wanted to try to stay far enough from the river and its habitations, but at the same time out of the wadis, so that I wasn't forever scrambling up and down.

By five in the morning I was starting to worry about finding somewhere to lie up for the day. At 0530 it was still fully dark, but when I came to the top of a cliff looking out over the river, something made me decide to scramble four or five metres down the face. There I found a ledge, and at the back of it a nice flat area, with a crack going back underneath the cliff. That seemed as good a hiding place as any, and I lay in it until day broke.

Monday 28 January: Escape – Day Five
When the light came up, I found I could look straight down into the river. On the opposite bank there was a small village. The houses were simple, single-storey structures, mostly built of breeze blocks, with

flat roofs. They stood in areas of dirt, with no sign of a garden. Soon, as I watched through binoculars, people started to come out and walk up and down, going about their daily tasks. There seemed to be very few men, but plenty of women, all dressed in black robes from head to foot and heavily veiled. Groups of them came down to the water's edge to fill their buckets. Surprise, surprise, the place was alive with dogs.

I was looking for any strange activity which might suggest that the area was on the alert – military vehicles driving about, or troops on the move, but I saw nothing of note.

Two men spent the whole day fishing, paddling up and down in a boat. On each pass they let themselves drift maybe a hundred metres downstream. The speed at which the boat picked up confirmed that the current was strong, and I felt glad that I hadn't tried to swim across. In daylight the water looked a dark brown colour, and a good deal of rubbish was floating about inside my bottle; but the sight of the shining fish reassured me. If they could live in the river, I thought, the water couldn't be too bad.

All that day – Monday 28 January – I lay on the ledge, with my webbing under my head as a pillow.

I felt secure, almost peaceful. It was the sort of place, I thought, in which an eagle or a peregrine falcon would nest. There was no movement close to me, and my main enemy was boredom. I spent hours studying my map, trying to work out exactly where I was. Again I managed to convince myself that I was well to the west of my true position, and a great deal nearer the border.

I tried not to think about food, but inevitably, with all that time on my hands, it had become a major preoccupation. Each one of those houses opposite had food in it, even if it was only flour or bread. If it weren't for the dogs, I could nip into one under cover of darkness and steal a loaf. In my mind I kept seeing the sachets of fruit that I'd left in my bergen. What wouldn't I give for some pineapple in syrup? *When I get out of here*, I thought, *I'm going to eat a gallon of ice cream*.

The day passed. From my perch on the cliff face, I watched the shadows lengthen in the village opposite. Gradually the grey-brown fields beyond the houses faded into the dusk. As evening came on, I wanted to get going again, and had to hold myself in check.

* * *

Monday 28 January: Escape – Night Five

When darkness fell at last, I moved out, climbed to the top of the cliff and started walking. That night, thank goodness, people disappeared into their houses and after dark there was nobody about. But to keep out of the way, I pushed up towards the wadis, between a line of pylons and the main road. Up there, I found myself in steep country. I kept coming to what looked like small quarries, so I'd have to climb down, walk across a flat floor, then scramble up again and along the top. It was really tiring, and my feet were seriously sore.

After studying the map all day, I thought I'd worked out where I was – a big bend in the river with a village on it. This looked only about a day's walk from the border – a fact which lifted my morale and gave me strength.

Again I walked all night. The occasional car went along the main supply route, which was three or four hundred metres down to my right. Some had headlights on, others were driving blind. At some point late in the night the headlights of a car illuminated a motorway-sized sign. I was too far away to read the names, but I decided to move down to the road and check what it said.

It was then that I saw the only wild animal in the whole of my trek. As I dropped towards the road I looked through the night-sight. There, on top of a mound, stood a big fox, staring down at me. I knew what he was from his sharp-pointed face and sticking-up ears. For a whole minute I watched him, and he never moved; then I went on, and left him in possession of his territory. In that fox I recognized a fellow creature of the night. I bet that, like me, he lay up all day and came out only when darkness fell. He can't have been as short of food as I was, but I found it hard to imagine what he lived on, because never in all my time on the move or lying up did I see any form of rodent.

Closing on the sign, I peered up at it. It was written in English as well as Arabic:

AL QAIM 50

NEW ANA 50

New Ana was behind me, and I'd known for some time that I was heading for Al Qaim – but fifty kilometres! I had thought I was almost there. That was a massive blow to my morale. Sitting there in despair, I thought, *I'm never going to finish this walk.* When I got out the map and pinpointed my position, I saw I was still eighty or ninety kilometres from the border – at least two days short of the spot I thought I'd reached.

I couldn't believe it. I felt as if I'd had a kick between the legs, and sat down on the side of the road, staring at the sign. But the evidence was there, and everything fitted together, as I worked out where I was and where I'd been. The reality was intensely depressing.

There was nothing for it but to keep going.

Weighed down by exhaustion, thirst and fear, I started moving along the line of the main supply route. I was only a hundred metres from it when I heard a drone from somewhere along the road behind me. I went to ground and lay listening. The noise was coming from miles away to the east, but it grew steadily until it seemed to fill the night. A four-ton wagon went past – but still the heavy drone was increasing. I moved down to the edge of the road and hid in some rocks, looking along the highway through the night-sight. For minutes I couldn't see anything. Still the noise built up.

Then, as I scanned for the twentieth time, I saw a black dot, which grew bigger and bigger until it became a massive vehicle, filling the sight. With a tremendous roar it came level, and suddenly

I realized I had a Scud missile going by me! The TEL vehicle was a huge articulated truck, with the missile canopied-up under tarpaulins on its trailer, and a convoy of smaller trucks behind it. They were all heading out towards the Syrian border. In one of them, with an open back, I could see a whole gang of soldiers.

That's what I'm here for, I thought to myself. *To find Scuds!* I never imagined I'd get as close to one as this. Should I have opened fire on it? I couldn't have destroyed the missile, but a grenade from the 203 into the front of the truck might have put the launcher off the road. I would have given away my position, though, and the guys in the convoy would have been on top of me.

If only I could report back what I'd seen: this was exactly the information the Coalition needed. I whipped out my TACBE, switched on and spoke into it, but as before I got no response. The Scud disappeared into the distance

On the move once more, I crossed the main supply route, so that I was between the road and the river, which at that point were maybe fifteen kilometres apart. Now the ground was really flat, and again I started crossing ploughed fields. It was time to look for a lying-up position, but here in the farmland I couldn't see any rough, broken areas. So I planned to move back across the road and regain the higher ground beyond. Then I came to a culvert – a tunnel underneath the highway about two metres high and three wide. It was obviously built for pedestrians and animals to walk through.

I was feeling so exhausted and let down that I decided to lie up in the tunnel. It was a bad decision, but I can see why I took it. I was thinking, *You're going down. You're not going to last much longer. Why not take a vehicle and drive to the border?* The culvert would make a good base for such a hijack.

I sat there in the tunnel having this discussion with myself. My lazy side was saying, *Just do it: grab a vehicle and drive out*. The other side was saying, *What happens if there's two people in it? How are you going to make them stop? What if there's only one man, and he just drives on? Once you've been seen and reported, that's you finished.*

I went through the scenario again and again. I imagined myself standing on the road, putting one hand up, levelling my weapon – and the car accelerating past. Then I'd have given my position away and lost all the advantages I'd so painfully built up. If Stan had still been with me, the idea would have been even more tempting – but even if we got a vehicle, the chances were that we'd drive into a control point.

I decided not to risk it. But I'd landed myself in a hell of a place. While I'd been dithering, the sky had begun to lighten, and it was already too late to move on. Safe or not, the place was very uncomfortable. The wind was blowing straight through that culvert like it came from the North Pole. Soon I was absolutely frozen. I tried moving rocks to make a little shelter, but the wind still whistled through the gaps. In the gloom I could see that bushes were growing in the floor of the tunnel, and I thought that maybe I could pile some into a barrier. But when I grabbed one, I got a handful of vicious thorns. There seemed to be no way of improving my shelter, so I simply lay down, determined to stick it out.

Just at full daylight, I heard the sound I wanted least in the world: goat bells. I'd had enough of goats and goatherds already. Looking through the tunnel towards the river, I saw the lead animal come into view, heading confidently into the culvert, obviously on its way through. I just had time to scoot out the other end of the tunnel and up the sloping embankment of the main supply route. As I ran towards the top of it, a car was approaching at speed, so I flung myself into a shallow ditch which led down the bank at an angle from the road-edge.

There I lay on my back, trapped, looking straight down over my boots to the top of the culvert exit. In a few seconds the lead goat emerged below me, not three metres away. More and more goats came into view, pushing and jostling. Their stink rose all round me. Last came the goatherd, an old man wearing a long, woolly coat over several other layers, with a white shamag wrapped round the top of his head. He was leading a donkey, which had a blanket over its back. Five or six dogs jostled at his heels. As he walked out, the top of his head was barely a metre below my boots.

I lay rigid, with the 203 down my front, praying that he would not look back and that the dogs wouldn't get wind of me. Had they done so, I'd have had to shoot him. I didn't want to kill an innocent civilian, but I was desperate. If I had shot him, I would have been in a dire position: I'd have had to run off into the wadi system with the pack of dogs after me, and even if I'd made a temporary getaway, the old man's death would have put down a great big marker. Obviously he came out that way every morning, and people would be expecting him back.

How the dogs failed to smell me, I still cannot imagine – unless my scent was obliterated by the stink of the goats. I held my breath as the party moved slowly away, up into the wadis. The old man never looked back, and the jingle of bells faded among the rocks.

I couldn't go back into the culvert, because it was clear that at some time during the day the flock and their keeper would return. Equally, I couldn't move down anywhere below the road, because the farmland was too open, and too full of people at work. Besides, I felt sure that there must be a village, or at least a few houses, not far off.

I lay still and watched the goats until they were out of sight. My mind was racing. There was only one way I could go – up into the wadis. But traffic had started to build up on the motorway; every other minute a vehicle came past, and if I began moving up onto the high ground, a driver might see me. I kept imagining what would happen if somebody spotted me and raised the alert. The hunt would be on, and because it was still just after dawn, the searchers would have all day to catch me.

I decided to take my chance and make a go for it between cars. I rolled over onto my belly, slung the 203 on my shoulder, slithered down the embankment and began crawling up the dry river bed. Every time I heard a car coming, I went to ground, scared stiff that I would be seen. After a hundred metres I scuttled upwards and got round into the beginning of the wadi system, maybe 500 metres from the road. Then I walked on again until I found a hollow in the ground, and lay down in that.

There I was, stuck again for the hours of daylight. It wasn't a very good hideout. Although I couldn't see the road, I had a reasonable view downhill maybe 200 metres, but behind me the outlook was blocked by a mound. If anyone had come along, I wouldn't have seen him until he was on top of me. This kept me fully on edge. Any sound made me whip round, even if it was only the wind passing over the rocks.

I calculated that this was Tuesday January 29, and a map check showed that I was still at least seventy kilometres from the border. Working backwards, I realized that due to hypothermia Stan and I had miscalculated on our last night together, and we'd gone in a much more northerly direction than we'd supposed.

By this stage, even keeping still had become painful. Because of the cold, I had to lie on one side or the other with my knees tucked up to my chest. I'd lost so much weight that my pressure points had become very sore.

I could see that the day was going to be a long one.

CHAPTER 10
ECHOES OF AFRICA

Tuesday 29 January: Escape – Day Six

There was something spooky about my surroundings. The wind blowing through the rocks of that huge wilderness took my mind back to another desert, another time. Africa . . . the Kalahari. My thoughts floated away to the time when 'B' Squadron was deployed on a three-month training exercise, my troop staff sergeant was killed, and we all became caught up in what felt like voodoo or black magic.

For the various parts of the exercise, the squadron had spread out over a wide area. The Air Troop went free-falling; the Boat Troop splashed around in the swamps; the Mobility Troop drove around the Kalahari desert; and the rest of us went climbing in the Tsodilo Hills. That was my first trip abroad with the squadron, and it brought home to me how dangerous our training was.

On our first evening in the country, before the troops split up, we had a lesson on snakes from an African called Lazarus. He started releasing snakes from a sack to show us the various kinds which we might come across.

He brought out a spitting cobra, holding it by the throat, and said that if you gripped it like that, it couldn't spit. 'Watch that thing,' growled the SQMS, 'because if it does spit, and the stuff gets in your eyes, you'll have problems.' Sure enough, as Lazarus came past me the cobra spat, and although I closed my eyes, some spit landed on my arm and the side of my face. I wiped it off immediately, but wherever a drop had touched me, it took the pigment out of my skin. I was left with pale dots all over my cheek, and a patch the shape of the British Isles on one arm.

As a grand finale Lazarus produced an Egyptian cobra – a massive creature about four metres long – which he set down on the ground. We were gathered round in a circle, and he said, 'Stand still, and let it go through your legs.' Everything was fine until one guy moved and the cobra chased him. The man ran up onto a water bowser, and the snake wrapped itself round one of the axles, baring its enormous fangs as Lazarus heaved on its tail, trying to drag it off. In the end he got it back into his sack, but it was amazing that none of us had been bitten.

After that little introduction, our troop moved up to the Tsodilo Hills. Our camp was maybe half an hour's walk from the base of the biggest hill – an outcrop of bare, blue-grey rock which rose in tiers from a dead-flat plain. Some of the tiers, which went up in vertical rock faces, were anywhere between thirty and sixty metres high. It looked like an enormous, sharp staircase.

In the evening, as we sat round the fire, one of the guys said, 'I'm going out shooting – does anyone fancy coming?' Nobody could be bothered. So he went out on his own, and presently he came back with a small, furry animal about the size of a hare.

A few Botswanan soldiers had been attached to us for training, and when he offered the animal to them, there was a big commotion. The Botswanans were with some Bushmen, who became very agitated. The little men raised a hubbub, rushed about and began lighting more fires. Via the Botswanans, the message came back to us strongly that we shouldn't kill any more animals. It was dangerous, they said, and would provoke the spirits who lived on the mountain.

Next morning we had a brief on the climb. Ian, our mountain guide, had worked out that rain was probably going to come in during the afternoon, so he told everybody to be off the rock by midday. Then he split us into climbing pairs, and sent us off. I was with Ian himself, and when we reached the first of the rock faces, he showed me how to use devices called 'friends'. These expand and lock themselves in position when you hammer them into crevices.

Joe Farragher – a staff sergeant and a big, heavy man of about 110 kg, strong as an ox – went off climbing with a guy called Trev, who soon stepped off a rock. Although Trev only fell about a metre, he put his back out and had to be carried all the way back to camp. As a replacement, Joe got a young officer to go climbing with him. By the time he left for his second attempt, it was already 11 a.m. and he shouldn't really have returned to the mountain, because everyone had been told to be off it by twelve.

Ian and I were climbing away when suddenly we heard yells from round the corner. It was the officer, shouting down that there'd been an accident. Ian got both of us down onto a ledge, and we hurried round. We found Joe lying on the rock. He had fallen about twenty-five metres. We ran up to him, and I tried breathing into his mouth to give him CPR. But there was frothy red blood coming out of his mouth, and when I touched the back of his head under his climbing helmet, it felt like a broken eggshell.

He was obviously dead.

We shouted down to some others to send for the Alouette helicopter, which was on stand-by.

Soon the chopper came in, but the ledge was too narrow for it to land, and the face of the mountain was so steep that the pilot had difficulty hovering close enough for a doctor to abseil down. The heli began rocking, so that the doctor was swinging in and out. If he'd missed the ledge, he'd have fallen over fifty metres. In the end, though, he got down safely.

After he'd pronounced Joe dead, we tied his body into an old stretcher and prepared to lower it down the face. The drop was so long that we had to tie two ropes together. Ian asked me to abseil down first, to make sure that we could get our figure-of-eight linking device past the knot. I was feeling quite shocked, but also excited to be involved in a real body retrieval. As I went over the edge, I wasn't sure where I was going to end up, but luckily it turned out that the knot was level with another flat ledge, so passing it was easy.

It should have taken no more than half an hour to get Joe down, but everything seemed to go wrong. Ropes kept getting snagged or broken, and several times the body nearly fell out of the stretcher. We had to keep tying him back in, and it was awful to see a person we had known and liked trussed up like a stuffed chicken. Like the rest of us he was wearing shorts and a T-shirt, and by the time we got him down he was in a mess, with his skin all scraped. Altogether we struggled for eight hours, and darkness was falling when we reached the plain.

That evening we were all pretty subdued, and we didn't feel any better the next day when the Alouette which flew the body out broke down. Then we heard that while the guys from the Air Troop had been free-falling, the engines of their C-130 had caught fire, and the aircraft was forced to land.

We were starting to wonder whether there was some jinx on the exercise when one of the Air Troop produced a paperback copy of the South African explorer Laurens van der Post's book about the Bushmen: *The Lost World of the Kalahari*.

'Listen to this,' he said, and he read out some passages describing how the author had come to this very area, maybe forty years before, in search of Bushmen. When members of his party killed an antelope and a warthog, everything went belly-up: wild bees attacked the camp at sunrise – not once, but every morning – even though it was highly unusual for them to fly at that time of day; when the expedition's cameraman tried to film some ancient cave paintings, the movie camera repeatedly broke down; their tape-recorder also ceased to function. In the end van der Post became so scared that he decided to leave the area immediately.

First, though, he got his guide, Samutchoso, to communicate with the spirits. After the man had gone into a trance, the answer came back: 'The spirits of the hills are very angry with you, so angry that if they had not known your intention in coming here was pure, they would long since have killed you. They are angry because you have come here with blood on your hands . . .'

To win forgiveness, van der Post wrote a letter addressed to 'The Spirits, The Tsodilo Hills', in which he humbly begged pardon. He promised to bury the note at the base of the great cave painting which he had found. He then got all his companions to sign the letter, sealed it in an envelope, and placed it in a lime juice bottle, which he duly buried in the cave. After that he had no more trouble: his Land Rovers started without difficulty, and the expedition moved on.

His experience sounded like our own, and the death of that one animal seemed to have put us under the same spell. We decided to go and look for the cave, and I walked around the mountain with one other guy, Merv. We found the cave easily enough. I thought it looked a bit creepy, and didn't fancy walking in; but Merv decided it was all right – so we went in, and at the back we found a green bottle, corked up, with a piece of paper inside.

Back at the camp, we reported on what we'd found. People made a few jokes, but Harry (an Everest climber, who had spent a lot of time in mountains, and felt sympathy for the people who lived in them) suggested that we should write a note of our own, apologizing for the death of the animal, put it in another bottle, and leave it in the cave.

When our message was ready, Merv and I went back to the cave with it. The old bottle was still there – but something very strange had happened. Although the cork was still in place, the paper inside had been shredded, as if by a hamster. Of course, we were spooked. Then we thought that some of our own guys must have been messing around. We left our bottle beside the first one, and went back to the camp – only to find that nobody else had been near the cave.

Whatever had happened, the atmosphere was becoming tense. Next morning we went up the mountain again and studied the place where Joe had fallen. Things somehow didn't look right. All three of Joe's 'friends' had come loose at once, but there seemed to be no reason for it. We sent for Ian, the expert. He agreed that the friends should never have come out.

By now everyone was becoming nervous. The place had an unpleasant atmosphere; we felt as though we were being watched. Even off the mountain, mishaps kept occurring. A herd of goats came through the camp and wrecked the tents, knocking everything over and chewing up our clothes. One of the Mobility Troop fell off his motorbike and broke his collarbone. The Boat Troop was attacked by a hippo, which bit off one of the twin tails of an inflatable boat. The bang scared the animal off, but the boat was finished. When the RAF flew a Hercules over the top of the mountain and tried to throw out a wreath for Joe, it blew back into the aircraft. So they flew over again, and twice more it came back in. You could, at a stretch, say it was because of air turbulence, but it seemed weird. Only when they were three or four miles from the mountain did the wreath finally stay out and float away.

All this could have been coincidence – but there was no doubt that the Bushmen believe in the power of the mountain spirits. By the end of the exercise I was well on the way to doing the same. I began to feel that there were forces at work which we simply didn't understand.

One of the guys came with me to consult a witch doctor in the nearby village and find out what fate had in store for us. After we'd dropped a few boxes of rations in payment, a skinny, middle-aged man wearing nothing but a loincloth came out of his mud hut carrying a small leather bag. He swept a patch of earth clear with one hand and tipped six or eight bones onto it. He sat staring at them for thirty seconds, muttering to himself. Through the Botswanan who was with us, the message came back that we had nothing more to worry about, and we started to feel happier.

With our squadron exercise finished, we drove away, and as I looked out of the back of the Land Rover at the mountain, I still had the feeling that there was something there, watching us, glad to see us go. We were told not to mention the story back in Hereford, for the sake of Joe's family. But that was the first incident for me in which I'd seen someone killed, and it stuck in my mind for ever.

Remembering Africa helped pass the day. But cold, hunger, thirst and the pain of lying on rock continually reminded me I was in Iraq. Somehow the hours dragged by. At about five in the afternoon I moved up to the top edge of the mound and lay there gazing into the distance. Ahead of me, in the direction I needed to go, ridges of bare rock rose one behind the other, greyer and greyer as they stretched to the horizon. Nearby the ground was rolling, and on my left hills climbed steeply towards a high plateau. Looking west, I could see an old stone fort perched on one of the ridges running up from the river valley; it was very high up, with excellent views all around. I worried slightly that it might be a manned border post, but somehow the sight of that man-made structure gave me a lift. At least it was different to the barren wastes of the desert.

I realized that as I grew weaker I was covering the ground more slowly, not making the progress I expected. All the same, after studying the map on and off during the day, I reckoned that one good night's march would take me across the border.

Then a simple event gave my morale a tremendous boost. Once again the goats came into view below me, and I held my breath as they grazed nearby. Then I saw their herder. Keeping well down behind a rock, I watched him. The goats wandered down the lower side of the mound, away from me, but the man whipped round my side of it, out of sight of the road. As I looked down, from about a hundred metres away, he whipped up his dishdash, squatted down and went to the toilet. Then, quick as a flash, he ran back to catch up with his flock.

Back with the squadron in Saudi Arabia, the SSM

had said something to me. 'You'll never see an Iraqi go to the toilet. They're very shy about it.' But here it was, happening right in front of me, and I lay there doubled up with silent laughter. *Wait till I get out of here!* I thought. *I'm going straight to the SSM to tell him what I've seen!*

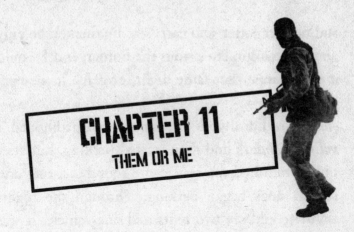

CHAPTER 11
THEM OR ME

Tuesday 29 January: Escape – Night Six

My morale had been down, but suddenly it was back up again. I couldn't stop laughing and wanted to get started.

I needed water urgently. On the map I'd found a pumping station, and I felt I must have a good chance of getting a drink there. Surely a pumping station would have clean water coming out of it? This was my sixth night on the run, and in six nights and six days I'd had nothing to eat but two packets of biscuits. I was seriously dehydrated, and my feet were in ribbons. Even so, I felt pretty good, and had that sense of excitement mixed with apprehension that you get before a race or a big football match.

All I had to do was go down to the pumping

station, get water, and carry on. By then I'd be only about ten kilometres from the border, and I would either cross it that same night, or reach it the next day.

Things didn't work out as easily as I had hoped. I waited till dark and then started walking, but after only a hundred metres I came round a corner and several dogs began barking. Through the night-sight I could see two tents and one vehicle. It was obviously a Bedouin encampment. But nobody came out for a look round, so I moved carefully away to the left, boxed the position and carried on.

As soon as I could, I swung down to the right, heading for the pumping station. I followed a line of telegraph poles, which made navigation easy. But by then my feet had become really sore, and I had to keep stopping. I forced myself to do 150 metres between rests. Every one of them was a major effort.

According to my map, I was heading for a point at which the telegraph lines crossed a run of pylons. In due course I saw the pylons, coming in on my right. The wadis to my left were getting deeper, the sides steeper. Then I saw that instead of crossing the telegraph line, the pylons were set out parallel with it. The map wasn't making sense, so I decided to just cut down to the right and head for the river.

I peeled off the high ground and started on another bearing, confident that I'd hit the river sooner or later. As I went down I spotted a square, white building with a flat roof – the pump house. Coming close, I saw that the end facing me was open, and that a lot of pipes ran in and out of it. There was one main pipe, which I guessed was bringing water from the river, and several smaller ones.

By then I seemed to have grown careless. Whether or not it was the result of exhaustion, I don't know. When you're that tired, it's all too easy to sling your weapon over your shoulder instead of carrying it at the ready, and just saunter along. Going from very cautious to careless happens gradually, without you noticing.

In any case, I walked straight into this place, lulled by the fact that it was silent and no machinery was working. I wasn't crash-banging about, but I didn't case the building as carefully as I might have. I even got my torch out and shone it around, because I could hear water dripping from a pipe. There it was – a steady drip, glistening in the torch beam.

Then, as I started getting my water bottle out, I

looked up and noticed a little glassed-in hatchway on the back wall, with a red glow coming through it. Standing up to peer through, I saw a small electric fire with a bar glowing. Across from it lay an Arab, huddled down in a parka and sleeping bag, asleep on a camp-bed. He was separated from me only by the thickness of the wall.

I cursed myself. What was I doing in this building anyway? I tiptoed out, without any water, and crept away. It took a fright like that to wake me up. Things had started to seem too easy. I was making good progress. The border was only a short distance ahead. Nobody had challenged me for a while, and I'd started to switch off my defence mechanisms.

Getting over the fright, I moved on in a state of maximum alert. I held my weapon at the ready, and moved very slowly, scanning constantly. But I was hardly clear of the pump house when, from high ground to my left, an air-raid siren went off. The noise started low, wound up to a high note, then swung down again. I hit the ground, thinking I had tripped some alarm, and lay there listening. Up and down went the metallic scream, high and low. As I searched through the night-sight, scanning the high ground, I made out anti-aircraft positions with gun barrels showing against the sky. Black figures were running around them. Then I saw tall towers, maybe fifty metres high, with what looked like cables slung between them. They seemed to be part of a communications network, and when I heard a drone start up, I thought the noise was coming from generators. I reckoned I'd walked into some sort of signals base. How had I got in among all this without seeing anything? I certainly hadn't crossed any fence or other barrier, but somehow I had landed in the middle of the complex.

I knew I wasn't far from the river. Vegetation started only a couple of hundred metres below me, and I thought that must mark the bank. I lay still until the all-clear went up – a noise like a Second World War siren – and everything quietened down. Whatever had caused the alert, it hadn't been me. When I reckoned it was safe to move, I got up and set off cautiously towards the river – only to see a group of five men walking towards me. Back on the ground, I lay still until they had passed and disappeared.

Even though I was desperate for water, I decided I had to get out of this thickly populated area.

I had seen from the map that the river bent round, and thought I could hit it at another point not far ahead. But now I seemed to be in the middle of numerous scattered positions, and I would have to weave my way through them.

I crept onwards. To my front I saw something sticking up into the sky. Peering through the night-sight, I realized that it was the barrel of an anti-aircraft gun. As I looked down, I saw the rest of the weapon right in front of me.

I pulled back, boxed it and moved on, threading my way forward between buildings which showed up here and there, pale in the moonlight. The place was extremely confusing, as it didn't seem to be laid out in any regular pattern. The dirt roads were neither straight nor at right-angles to each other, but coming in from all directions. On the ground, insulated land-lines were running all over the place. I thought of cutting them, to put local communications out of action, but knew that it would only draw attention to my presence.

My map was far too large-scale to show details that would have been useful to me, and it no longer bore any relation to the ground. At one point I could see a big cliff coming round in front of me, like the wall of a quarry – but of course there was no sign of that on my sheet.

Then – wonder of wonders – I reached a stream, with vegetation growing beside it. The water looked crystal clear, and the moonlight shone through it onto a white bottom. I thought, *I'm in luck here. A spring of clean water, flowing down into the Euphrates.* The whole place was so dangerous that I didn't go down for a drink; I just filled my bottles, popped them into my side-pouches, and moved quickly away.

Just as I left the stream I saw a file of seven men walk across my front, two or three paces apart. They were moving carefully, obviously on patrol. I froze, thinking, *If they've got a dog, it's going to pick up my scent now.* But no – they disappeared, and I moved out on a bearing, going very slowly.

Again I came across an anti-aircraft position. This time I was so close that I peered over a wall of sandbags and saw three men lying on the ground in sleeping bags. I felt a surge of fear, rising like acid from stomach to throat. The thought flashed into my mind that if I'd had a silenced weapon, I could at least have taken out anyone who spotted me. But nobody had: the men were all asleep, and within a few seconds I was creeping slowly away.

The next thing I hit was a laager point – a circle of vehicles defending some position. Mounds of rock or minerals stood about – it looked like a quarry. As I came creeping round the side, I walked right up to a Russian-made Gaz 80 jeep, only four or five metres away. Again I got a bad fright. I couldn't see through the vehicle's windows; for all I knew it could have been full of people. For a few seconds I held my breath, 203 levelled, waiting for it to erupt.

When nothing happened, I turned to go back. I found I'd passed other vehicles and wandered into the middle of this park without seeing it. There were four-ton trucks with the canvas backs off, some with the canvas on, buses and double-deck car transporters. None of them had armour or weapons fitted, but this was a big collection of general transport. How I'd penetrated in among all these without noticing them, I couldn't explain. With hindsight, I realize that my concentration was coming and going, functioning one moment but not the next. At the time I just felt confused.

No matter how I'd got in there, I *had* to get out. Ahead of me were houses, with light coming from one window. Silhouetted figures were moving across it, and I could hear voices calling. I pushed off to the right, sometimes walking on tiptoe, often crawling on hands and knees.

I boxed that particular group of buildings. Then, ahead of me, lay a single big, whitewashed house with a steeply pitched roof and a pale-coloured wall. To the left were two other buildings with lights shining from them and people outside, talking and shouting. I think there was also music playing on a radio.

The big house was easily the most impressive I'd seen, and by far the best maintained. High on one wall was a large portrait of Saddam Hussein. It showed the dictator bare-headed, wearing military insignia on his epaulettes. For several seconds I stood looking at it, thinking, *You're definitely in the wrong place now, mate!* What made me stand there gawping, I can't explain. Again, as in the pumping station, I seemed to have grown blasé. After surviving so many close encounters, I felt that nobody could see me, and I needn't be so careful any more.

As I stood there, a man came round the corner, only fifty metres away – a dark figure, silhouetted against the light. I felt a surge of fear, but instead of bolting I simply turned away and walked casually round the side of the house. In two steps I was out of sight.

Then I ran.

As I sprinted, I told myself, *For God's sake, get a grip*.

The man had seen me. I knew that. But he didn't seem to have followed up. Round the back of the building I spotted a ditch running along the side of the road. I dived into it, and as I lay there two family-type vehicles came rolling down. The big house suddenly burst into life: security lights blazed on, and people poured out to meet them. A man got out of the vehicle, and four of the other guys body-guarded him into the house. As soon as the party was inside, the lights went off, so that the place was plunged into darkness again. It crossed my mind that this could be Saddam himself. The house was an impressive one, and well maintained. Was this his secret hideaway? Then I realized that he would never draw attention to himself by having his own portrait on the wall; more likely, this was the home of the local governor, or some similar official.

I seemed to have strayed into a nightmare, with unexplained people and events popping up all over the place. By now I'd been in this complex – whatever it was – for five hours, trying to find my way out. Time was cracking on.

According to my route plan, I should already have been on the border. Something had gone wrong with my map-reading. It looked like I would have to lie up without food for yet another day. Oddly enough, I never felt desperate with hunger, never got pains in the stomach. My biggest worry was that I was gradually growing weaker – less able to walk, less able to concentrate.

My immediate plan was to creep back up to the road and go somewhere beyond it, clear of the buildings, so that I could sneak another look at the map. But before I could move, I heard footsteps and voices coming down the path towards me. By the sound of it, there were two men at least. I was crouching in a corner beside a mound, without cover, and they were coming right on top of me.

My survival instinct took over – instinct sharpened by years of training. Whoever these guys were, it was going to be them or me.

To fire a shot in that position would have been fatal, so I quietly laid my 203 down and got my knife open in my right hand.

As the first man came level with me I grabbed him

and quickly cut his throat. He went down without a sound.

When the second man saw me, his eyes widened in terror and he began to run. But somehow, with a surge of adrenalin, I flew after him, jumped on him and brought him down with my legs locked round his hips. I got one arm round his neck in a judo hold and stretched his chin up. There was a muffled crack as his neck broke, and he died immediately.

I could feel hot, sticky blood all down my front. There hadn't been a sound. Now I had two bodies to dispose of. To leave them where they were would let everyone know I was there. But if they just went missing, the chances were that nobody would raise the alarm for a few hours at least.

Luckily the river was less than a hundred metres off, and a gentle slope covered by small, loose rocks led down to it. Luckier still, the bank was screened by a stand of tall grass. Each body made a scraping, rattling noise as I dragged it over the rocks; but I got both to the edge of the water, one at a time, without anyone seeing me. Then I loaded them up with stones inside their shirts, dragged them into the water and let them go.

Knowing my bottles were full, I didn't bother to

drink any of the dirty water in the river. I was on high alert, and it had taken an hour to get rid of the bodies.

I *had* to clear the complex before daylight.

CHAPTER 12
OVER THE BORDER

Wednesday 30 January: Escape – Day Seven

Moving silently, I worked my way up to a road. Under it I found a culvert, and I thought I'd crawl into it for a look at my map. But as I came to the end of the tunnel, I heard a kind of growling. Thinking there must be some animal under the road, I tiptoed forward and peered into the pitch darkness. I couldn't see a thing. Suddenly I worked out what the noise was: it was some local, snoring. I felt slightly annoyed that an Arab had already nicked the hiding place I wanted. He was probably a soldier, and supposed to be on lookout duty. Lucky for me, then, that he'd decided to have a kip. Creeping back out, I climbed up on the side of the road and crossed over.

As I did that, I heard a shout from down by the houses where I'd heard people talking. I didn't think the yell had anything to do with me, but I ran across the road, made about fifty metres into the rocks and dropped down.

A man came running up the road, which was raised about two metres above the ground. He stopped right opposite me and stood staring in my direction. Evidently he couldn't see anything, and he ran back. A moment later, a blacked-out Land Cruiser roared past, its engine screaming in second gear, straight up the road to the junction with the main supply route, and disappeared.

For nearly half an hour I lay still, letting things settle. I felt drained of strength, but I couldn't stay where I was, so I began to work my way round the rocks. On my left was a run of chain-link fencing, quite high. So that side of the complex was protected, anyway.

Coming to a corner of the barrier, I went up onto the main supply route and crossed over. As I did so, I looked to my left and saw three guys manning a vehicle control point. Dodging back up a wadi, I peeped over the side and saw a line of anti-aircraft positions facing towards the Syrian border.

I pulled back again, stuck. The ground there was almost flat. I couldn't go forward, and I couldn't go back. Dawn was approaching. My only possible hiding place was another of the culverts under the road. I found three tunnels, each about the diameter of a forty-five gallon drum and maybe ten metres long. The first looked clean, and I thought that in daylight anybody looking in one end would see straight through it. The second seemed to be full of dead bushes and rubbish, so I crawled in and lay down.

In the confined space, I realized how badly I was stinking. But my surroundings were no better: there was a powerful stench of decomposing rubbish and excrement.

I was desperate for a drink. But when I went to compress the plastic clip that held the buckle on my webbing pouch, I found that my fingers were so sore and clumsy that I could scarcely manage the simple task. Gasping with pain, I used all my strength to force the clips together.

Then came a horrendous disappointment.

Bringing out one bottle at last, I opened it and raised it to my lips – but the first mouthful made me gasp and choke.

Poison!

The water tasted like acid. I spat it straight out, but the inside of my mouth had gone dry, and I was left with a burning sensation all over my tongue and gums. I whipped out my compass-mirror, pointed the torch-beam into my mouth and looked round it. Everything seemed all right, so I took another sip, but it was just the same. I remembered that when Stan had collapsed during the first night on the run I'd put rehydration powder into my bottles, to bring him round, and I wondered if the remains of it had somehow gone off.

I tried the second bottle. It was exactly the same. I couldn't make out what had gone wrong. Whatever the problem, the water was undrinkable, and I emptied the bottles out.

Now I'm done for, I thought.

I was in a really bad state.

It was eight days since I'd had a hot meal, two days and a night since I'd had a drink.

My tongue was completely dry; it felt like a piece of old leather stuck in the back of my throat.

My teeth had all come loose; if I closed my mouth and sucked hard, I could taste blood coming from my shrunken gums.

I knew my feet were in bits, but I didn't dare take my boots off, because I feared I'd never get them on again.

As for my hands – I could see and smell them all too well. The thin leather of my gloves had cracked and split, from being repeatedly soaked and dried out again, so that my fingers hadn't had much protection. I'd lost most of the feeling in the tips, and I seemed to have got dirt pushed deep under my nails, so infection had set in. Whenever I squeezed a nail, pus came out, and this stench was repulsive.

I wondered what internal damage I might be suffering, and could only hope that no permanent harm would be done. With the complete lack of food, I'd had no bowel movement since going on the run, and I couldn't remember when I'd last wanted to pee.

I yearned for food, of course, but more for drink – and when I did think about food, it was sweet, slushy things that I craved. If ever I found myself back among ration packs, I would rip into the pears in syrup, ice cream and chocolate sauce.

I felt very frightened. First and most obvious was the danger of being captured – the fear of torture, and of giving away secrets that might betray other guys from the Regiment. Almost worse, though, was the fact that I could see and feel my body going down so fast. If I didn't reach the border soon, I would be too weak to carry on.

Twisting round in the cramped space of the drain, I got out my map and tried for the hundredth time to work out where I was. It was now the morning of Wednesday 30 January. What options were left to me? Already light was coming up, and whatever happened, I was stuck in the culvert for that day. When dark fell again, I could try to sneak back down to the river, cross over and go along the other side – but it seemed a far-fetched hope. In any case, I was terrified of going anywhere near the river. Every time I'd tried it, something had gone wrong. One more attempt, and I might easily be captured. How long could I hold out? I just couldn't tell what my body was still capable of.

First, I somehow had to get through eleven hours of daylight – eleven hours, when every waking minute was agony. At least I was out of the wind, and less cold, so that I could drop off to sleep.

I started dreaming, usually about the squadron. I was with the rest of the guys. They were all around me, talking and laughing, getting ready to go. We didn't seem to be in any particular place, but their presence was completely real. Then suddenly, maybe ten minutes later, I'd wake up, shuddering violently, hoping against hope that my mates were still there, and fully expecting that they would be. Then I'd open my eyes and realize that I was alone in the culvert with no one to talk to. It was a horrible letdown.

I wasn't worried by the occasional rumble of a car going past above me, but soon I began to hear other movement: scurrying, scuffling noises, as if troops were running around. I thought, *Here we go. The next thing is going to be somebody at either end of this culvert, and I'll be caught like a rat in a drainpipe.*

From the scrabbling, it sounded as though soldiers' boots were moving everywhere. I reckoned that the bodies of the men I'd killed had been discovered, the alarm had gone up, and a search party was closing in on me.

Most of the noise was coming from the end towards which my feet were pointing. I tried to turn my 203 in that direction, but the drain was too narrow and I couldn't bring the weapon to bear.

Now was the moment I needed a pistol, or better still a silenced one.

The scrabbling noise came closer.

I tensed myself, certain that a man would stick his head into the end of the pipe at any second. If he did, my only option would be to try to scuttle out the other end . . .

But what did the intruder turn out to be? A goat! A herd was being driven up the side of the road. I watched their legs move steadily past. The scrabble of their feet on rocks, echoing through the tunnel, sounded like a whole company of soldiers on the move. Again I was terrified that they might have a dog with them; if they did, it would surely get my scent.

Tortured by thirst and by noises close at hand, I somehow stuck out the day. That was the lowest point of my whole escape. I'd lost so much weight that lying down became ever more agonizing. However I lay, my bones seemed to be sticking out, with no padding to cover them, and every five or six minutes I'd be in such discomfort that I'd have to turn over. Spine, hips, ribs, knees, elbows, shoulders – everything hurt, and I was developing sores all over. I kept telling myself, *You've got to clear that border tonight, whatever happens.* But first I somehow had to escape from the trap in which I'd landed myself – and if the night turned out clear again, I didn't see how I was going to avoid the vehicle control point.

Eventually darkness fell. When I poked my head out of the end of the culvert, my morale took a lift again. Until then the nights had been clear, but this one was black as pitch, with the sky full of storm clouds that looked so threatening I even thought it might rain. The very idea of moisture was exciting. If rain did come, and I turned up my face, at least my parched mouth would get some refreshment. Maybe I could even collect water by spreading out my map case.

Wednesday 30 January: Escape – Night Seven
I crept outside. The night was so dark that when I looked in the direction of the vehicle control point, I couldn't make it out. Moving closer, I found that the guards were still standing there, so I eased away until I could no longer see them, and when I was halfway between them and the anti-aircraft positions, I started walking at full speed.

Thank God for the darkness. Behind me nobody

moved, and I got clean away. I'd been going for nearly two hours, parallel with a road, when all of a sudden a blinding flash split the darkness. Convinced I'd walked into ambush lights, I flung myself down. But then from behind me came a heavy explosion, and I realized that an air raid was hitting the installation I'd just left. The same thing happened twice more: a flash, and a few seconds later a really big, deep boom. I kept thinking, *If this hadn't been a dark night, that's where I'd still be.* What effect the bombs were having I couldn't tell, but the explosions sounded colossal, and I thanked my lucky stars that I'd been able to move on.

Occasionally, far away to my left, I saw anti-aircraft fire going up into the sky, and I guessed it must be coming from the airfields we'd been told about at the beginning of our mission: H1 and H2. They were too far away for me to hear any noise, but I saw arches of tracer fire. At least it meant that the bases were under Coalition attack. I knew that 'A' and 'D' Squadrons were operating in that area, and I hoped it was they who were hammering the Iraqis.

I knew from the map that the Iraqi town of Krabilah should be coming up on my right.

Krabilah lay on the border, and there was a Syrian town beyond the frontier. The thought of it kept me going, but only just. By now my feet were so bad that whenever I sat down for a rest they went from numb to excruciating. Upright, I couldn't feel them much; sitting, I thought they were going to burst. Several times I sat there thinking, *I can't take much more of this*. Then the pain would ease off, and I had a few minutes of bliss, with nothing hurting.

The worst bit came whenever I stood up again, and the pain just exploded. Starting off, I couldn't help gasping with the sheer agony. I had to shuffle my boots along the ground, and I kept thinking, *If anyone sees me doddering along like this, I'll look a right idiot*. It wasn't till I'd taken about ten paces that my feet seemed to go numb again, and I could walk out. Occasionally I'd hit a sharp stone or rock – and boy, was that sore.

Never in my life had I been so exhausted. Often on selection and afterwards, I thought I had pushed myself to my limit – but this was something else. All I wanted to do was stop and rest, but I knew that if I did I would never reach the border before my body gave out.

Towards the end I was stopping and resting on my

feet. Because they were so agonizing if I sat down, I took to reading my map standing up – which was not a good idea, as my torch was up in the air instead of close to the ground. I'd walk until I was really knackered, then prop myself against something so that I kept the pressure on my feet.

I was so far gone that when I reached some houses I was on the point of giving in. *If only I were in England!* I thought. *There'd be milk bottles standing on the doorstep, and a milk-float coming past in the morning.* How many bottles of milk could I have drunk straight down?

I watched the houses for a while. They were only small places, but I'd find water in them, for sure, and food. Suddenly I decided I'd had enough. *I'll go in*, I thought, *and if I have to, I'll do the people in there. I'll get something to drink and take their vehicle.*

I slid along one side of the nearest house, and found a window in the wall. It had iron bars down it, with a hessian curtain inside. Music was being played inside the room, and a candle or oil-lamp was flickering. I went past the window and reached the front of the building. Outside the door stood a car. *Now!* I thought. *Just let the keys be in it!*

As I came round the corner I looked down,

and there was a dog, lying outside the door. The moment I saw it, it saw me and went berserk, barking frantically. Back I scuttled, along the side of the house, and away off into the wadis. The dog came out, and more dogs from the other buildings joined it. They followed me for about a hundred metres, barking like lunatics, then stopped.

Up in the wadis, I came to a railway line, scrabbled through a culvert under it, and was back in the desert. With a jolt I realized that this must be the same railway that Stan and I had crossed all those nights earlier. If only we'd tabbed straight along it, we'd have been out of Iraq days ago.

Spurred on by my latest fright, I kept walking, walking, walking. According to my calculations, I should have been passing Krabilah on my right, but there was no sign of the town. What I didn't realize was that every house had been blacked out because of the war, and that I had already gone clean by the place in the dark.

I reached a refuse heap, where loads of burned-out old cans had been dumped in the desert, and sat down among them to do yet another map study. I couldn't work things out. Where was the town? Above all, where was the Syrian border?

I started walking again, and as I came over a rise I saw three small buildings to my front. With the naked eye I could just make them out: three square bulks, blacked out. But when I looked through the night-sight, I saw chinks of light escaping between the tops of the walls and the roofs. As I sat watching, one person came out, walked round behind, reappeared and went back indoors. I was so desperate for water that I went straight towards the houses. Again I was prepared to take out one of the inhabitants if need be. I was only fifty metres away when I checked through the night-sight again and realized that the buildings were not houses at all, but sandbagged sangars with wriggly tin roofs. They formed some sort of command post, and were undoubtedly full of soldiers. Pulling slowly back, I went round the side and, sure enough, came on a battery of four anti-aircraft positions.

If I'd walked up and opened one of the doors, I'd almost certainly have been captured. Once more the fright got my adrenalin going and revived me.

On I stumbled for another hour. My dehydration was making me choke and gag. My throat seemed to have gone solid, and when I scraped my tongue, white fur came off it. I felt myself growing weaker by the minute. My 203 was so heavy it felt like it was made of lead. My legs had lost their spring and grown stiff and clumsy. My ability to think clearly had dwindled away.

At last I came to a point from which I could see the lights of a town, far out on the horizon. Something seemed to be wrong. Surely that couldn't be Krabilah, such a long distance off? My heart sank: was the border still so far away? Or was the glow I could see that of Abu Kamal, the first town inside Syria? If so, where was Krabilah? According to the map, Krabilah had a communications tower, but Abu Kamal didn't. The far-off town did have a bright red light flashing, as if from a tower – and that made me all the more certain that the place in the distance was Krabilah.

My morale plummeted once more. Like my body, my mind was losing its grip. What I could make out was some kind of straight black line, running all the way across my front. Off to my left I could see a mound with a big command post on it, sprouting masts. Closer to me were a few buildings, blacked out, but not looking like a town.

I sat down some 500 metres short of the black line and studied the set-up through the night-sight.

Things didn't add up. With Krabilah so far ahead, this could hardly be the border. Yet it looked like one. I wondered whether it was some barrier which the Iraqis had built because of the war, to keep people back from the border itself.

Whatever this line ahead of me might be, all I wanted to do was get across it. I forced myself to hold back, though, to sit down and observe it. *This is where you're going to stumble if you don't watch out*, I told myself. *This is where you'll fall down. Take your time.*

There I sat, shivering, watching, waiting. A vehicle came out of the command post and drove down along the line. Directly opposite my vantage-point two men emerged from an observation post, walked up to the car, spoke to the driver, jumped in, and drove off to the right. It looked as if the Iraqis were putting out roving observers to keep an eye on the border. I couldn't tell whether this was routine, or whether they suspected that enemy soldiers were in the area. After a few minutes I decided that the coast was clear, and I had to move.

At long last I came down to the black line. Creeping cautiously towards it, I found it was a barrier of barbed wire: three coils in the bottom row, two on top of them, and one on top of that. I had no pliers to cut with, so I tried to squeeze my way through the coils. It was impossible. Barbs hooked into my clothes and skin and held me fast. I unhooked myself with difficulty, and decided that the only way to go was over the top.

Luckily the builders had made the mistake, every twenty-five metres, of putting in three posts close to each other and linking them together with barbed wire. Obviously the idea was to brace the barrier, but the posts created a kind of bridge across the middle of the coils. I took off my webbing and threw it over, then went up and over myself. I cut myself in a few places, but it was nothing serious.

I couldn't believe I was clear of Iraq. The barrier seemed so insignificant that I thought it must only be marking some false or inner border, and that I would come to the true frontier some distance further on. The real thing, I thought, would be a big anti-tank berm, constructed so that vehicles could not drive across. Maybe this was why I had no feeling of elation. I felt nothing except utter exhaustion.

With my webbing back in place, I set off yet again on the same bearing. Never in my life, before or since, have I pushed myself so hard. I think I was brain-dead that night, walking in neutral, moving automatically, stumbling grimly onwards.

In the end I could go no further. I simply had to sit down and rest. I took my weapon off my shoulder, and just as I was lifting the night-sight from where it hung round my neck, I seemed to click my head, and felt what I can only describe as a huge electric shock. I heard a noise like a ferocious short-circuit – *krrrrrrrrk* – and when I looked down at my hands, there was a big white flash.

The next thing I knew I was sitting in the same place, but I couldn't tell if I had been asleep, or unconscious, or what. Time had passed, but I didn't know what had happened to me.

I got my kit back on and stood up. This time my feet were real torture, and I was barely able to totter forwards until they went numb again.

It was still dark. The night seemed very long.

Nothing for it but to keep going.

Was I in Syria or Iraq?

Couldn't tell . . .

Better steer clear of the odd house then, because each one had a dog.

What would I do when it got light?

Didn't know . . .

Couldn't think . . .

Should be in Syria . . .

I woke up a bit when I found I was crossing vehicle tracks. Then after a while I thought I heard something behind me. As I turned to look, the same thing happened: a big crack of static in the head and a blinding flash. This time I woke up on the ground, face-down.

On my feet again, I checked my weapon to make sure I hadn't pushed the muzzle into the ground as I fell, and went forward once more. Now I was walking towards a red light, which never seemed to get any brighter.

Things were becoming blurred now.

I was in and out of wadis, staggering on.

Then I was on a flat area with more tracks.

Then I came to the wall of one wadi and had another attack: a big crack in my head, the same *krrrrrk* of static, a flash . . .

The next thing I knew, I came round to find my nose blocked and aching. I couldn't tell how long I'd been unconscious, but dawn had broken, so I presumed that an hour had gone by, at least. In my compass-mirror I saw that blood had run down my cheeks and neck, matting in the stubble. Somehow I'd fallen flat on my face.

I propped myself against the rock wall. If ever I had come close to dying, it was then. I seemed to have nothing left. My strength had gone, and with it the will to move. I lay back with my head resting against the rock, feeling almost drunk.

Now that daylight had come, I knew I ought to lie up. But no – I couldn't last another day without water. For minutes I sat there in a heap. Then I got out my precious flask and drank the last little sip of whisky. It tasted horrible, like fire. I was so dehydrated that it burned all the way down into my stomach, and left me gasping and desperate. I wished I'd never drunk it.

Then suddenly, to my indescribable relief, out of the wadi wall came Paul, a member of the Bravo One Zero unit. He was dressed in green DPM, not desert gear, and he stopped about seven metres away from me.

'Come on, Chris,' he said, 'hurry up. The squadron's waiting for you.'

It seemed perfectly normal that the squadron should be there. Painfully I levered myself to my feet with the 203 and shuffled down the wadi, expecting to see the rest of the guys lined up, sorting themselves out, ready for the off.

Of course, when I came round the corner, there was nobody in sight.

To this day I swear I saw Paul walk out in front of me. I even heard the sound of his boots as he came towards me over the gravel in the wadi bed, and for a few moments I thought my nightmare was over. I thought help and salvation had come.

Far from it. It was just a hallucination. My mind was playing tricks on me. I was still on my own. It was another crippling blow to my morale. I sat down, trying to get myself together.

It was early morning on Thursday 31 January.

I'd been on the run for seven days and nights.

It was ten days since my last proper meal.

Six days since I'd finished my biscuits.

Three since I'd had any water.

My body wasn't going to last another day . . .

In a futile gesture I pulled out my TACBE, switched it on and let it bleep away. Then I looked up and realized that about a kilometre away there was a barn or house – a combination of both, standing out on a rise in the middle of scruffy fields in which rocks poked up out of the bare grey earth.

As I stood watching, a man came out of the house and walked away with a herd of goats. The people living in that barn must have water. I decided that I had to get some, whatever the cost. If I was in Syria, the people might be friendly. If I was still in Iraq, I was going to have to threaten to kill them, get a drink, and carry on.

I'd made up my mind: I was going in there, and I'd kill everybody if need be.

CHAPTER 13
SAFE OR SORRY?

Thursday 31 January: Escape – Day Eight
I closed in on the barn.

The building was made of dirty-white stone, with a low wall running out of its right-hand end. The doorway was open. Outside it was a young woman with a black scarf tied round her head in a band. She was bending over a wood fire and cooking pieces of dough over what looked like an upturned wok. Two or three children were playing in the open.

The woman saw me coming but did not react much. As I approached, my weapon in my hands, she lifted her head and called into the house. I was only five or six metres off when a young man came out. He looked about eighteen and had dark curly hair. He touched his chest and then his forehead with his right hand – a typical Arab greeting.

I went up and shook his hand, and pointed at the ground, asking, 'Syria? Is this Syria?'

He nodded, repeating, 'Seeria! Seeria!' Then he pointed over my shoulder and said, 'Iraq. Iraq.'

I looked back the way he was gesturing, and in the distance behind me, over the mounds to the east, I saw a town with a mast. Krabilah! Looking westward, I saw another town, also with a mast. Abu Kamal! The one to the east was miles behind me. Both towns had masts. I realized that I must have passed Krabilah early in the night, and that most of the walking I'd done since then had been unnecessary – nothing but self-inflicted torture. That line of barbed wire had been the frontier after all.

I'd been in Syria for hours.

The young man could see the state I was in. A worried look came over his face, and he began touching my hands. He took me by the sleeve and drew me into the barn. In the middle was a round oil stove with a glass door and a metal chimney that rose straight through the roof. At the far end of the room lay rolls of bedding and some straw. There was practically no furniture, and it was obvious the people were very poor. A woman with tattoos on her face sat breast-feeding a baby, and did not move as I came in.

I sat on a mat on the ground next to the stove with my weapon laid across my lap. The young man looked at me and asked in gestures if I wanted something to eat.

'Water!' I croaked, tipping up an imaginary glass. 'Water!'

A moment later he handed me a shiny metal bowl full of water, which tasted incredibly fresh and cold. Never in my life had I had a more delicious drink. I tipped it straight down my neck. The boy brought another bowlful, and I drank that as well. Next he gave me a cup of sweet tea, thick with dissolved sugar, and I put that down too. Then the woman came in with some of the bread she'd been making, and gave me a piece. It was still hot, and smelled delicious, but when I bit off a mouthful and tried to swallow it, it locked in my throat and would not go down.

I had to get my boots off. It was four days since I'd seen my feet, and I was dreading what I would find. As I undid the laces and eased the boots off, the stink was repulsive. Like my hands, my feet were rotting. I smelled as if my whole body was putrefying.

When the man saw the state of my feet, with pus oozing along the sides, he let out a yell. The woman who'd been cooking brought me over a wide bowl full of cold water and began to wash my feet. All my toenails had come off, and I couldn't feel my toes. But the water stung the rest of my feet like fire.

In spite of the pain, I forced myself to scrape the pus out of the cuts along the sides and round the heels. I also washed the blood off my face. With that done, it was bliss to lie back with my bare feet raised to the warmth of the stove and let them breathe. Another girl appeared from outside, took my socks and rinsed them through. When she brought them back they were still wet, but I pulled them on, and got my boots back on as well.

In sign language, and by making aircraft sounds, I tried to explain that I was a pilot and had been in a crash. Then I made some siren sounds – *dee-dah*, *dee-dah*, *dee-dah* – to show that I wanted to go to the police. A boy of about six had been drawing pictures of tanks and aircraft on sheets of dirty white paper. With my numb fingers I drew a police car with a blue lamp on the roof. Suddenly the message got through: the young man nodded vigorously and pointed towards the distant town.

'Go to the town?' I suggested, and I made driving motions. 'You have a vehicle?'

Again he nodded and pointed. What he meant, I soon found out, was that we should start walking down the road towards the town and hitch a lift.

With the water and tea inside me, my body seemed to have switched back on. I felt sharp again, as if there was nothing wrong, as if I could do the whole walk again. Everything seemed so relaxed that for a while I just sat there, recovering.

The old man came back with his goats and stood looking at me. Then, to get some action, I dug a sovereign out of my belt and showed it round. I started saying '*Felous, felous*' – 'money, money'.

As soon as he saw the gold, the young man clearly wanted to go into town. Maybe he thought that if he took me in I would give him the money. Soon everyone was staring at the sovereign. Another girl came in, and somehow I knew she said, 'He's got more on him somewhere.'

The old man appeared with a gun – some ancient hunting rifle. 'More,' he said. 'More.' By gestures he showed he wanted another coin, to make the girl a pair of earrings. Then he started demanding gold for the other girls as well.

'No, no, no,' I said. 'This is for goats, clothes and stuff. No more.'

The Arabs began muttering to each other. For half an hour things remained tense. I lay with my feet against the oil fire, warming up. It was the first time in a week that I hadn't felt half frozen. I had begun to hope that I could sleep in the farmhouse that night. But the young man had become determined to go into town, and indicated that I should come outside.

I decided not to wait any longer. To look less aggressive, I took off my webbing and smock, so I was left wearing my dark green jersey and camouflage trousers. Using sign language, I asked the man for some sort of bag. He produced a white plastic fertilizer sack, and I put my kit into that. I slung the sack over my shoulder and we set off along the dirt road.

Then I thought, *It's hardly the thing, to walk into a civilian town carrying a rifle.* So after we'd gone about two hundred metres, I broke my weapon down in two and put it in the bag. I still had my knife, but in this situation I could have done with a weapon that was easy to hide, like a pistol.

The young man was walking quite fast and I shuffled behind him, in too much pain to move quickly. Every minute or two he stopped and waited for me to catch up. Then, seeing I was in difficulties, he took the bag off me, and without the weight I made better progress.

'Tractor?' I kept saying. 'Where's a tractor?'

He answered me in Arabic. I think he was saying, 'One'll come soon.'

Wagons were rolling out from the town, and after a while one of them stopped. It was a Land Cruiser loaded with bales of hay. The driver could speak a little broken English. He said he was a camel farmer, and asked who I was.

'My aircraft's crashed,' I told him.

'Your aircraft? Where is it?'

'Over the hill, over there. I need to go to the police.'

'OK. I'll take you.'

He swung his vehicle round, and I got into the middle of the front seat, between him and the young man. I soon regretted it, though, because he started making aggressive comments. 'You shouldn't be here,' he said. 'This is our country. This is a bad war.'

'Yeah, I know,' I replied, and kept as quiet as possible.

When we hit the edge of town, I couldn't hide my disappointment. I'd been imagining a fairly built-up place, with banks and shops. There was nothing here but crude houses made of grey breeze blocks, with heaps of rubbish lying round them. No vegetation. No sign of gardens. Burned-out cars in the streets. To my surprise, the Syrians looked quite European. I even saw two men with flaming, carrot-coloured hair, one of them with a red beard.

My driver pulled up outside a house on the left-hand side of the road and beeped his horn. Out came an Arab dressed in a black dishdash. They spoke, then the driver said something to the young farm lad, who got out of the truck. He looked frightened, but I felt helpless because I didn't know what was happening.

'Everything all right?' I asked, but the driver spoke sharply to the lad, who set off walking, back towards his home.

The two of us went on into town, and the driver started having a go at me again. 'You want to go back to Iraq?' he said, and roared with laughter. 'I should take you back.'

'No, no!' I said. I brought out the letter, written in Arabic as well as English, that promised £5,000 to anyone who handed me safely back to the Coalition. The driver snatched it and began to stuff it into his pocket, as if it was actual cash.

'You don't understand,' I said. 'I have to be with this piece of paper. Me and the paper at the same time. You only get the money if the two are together.' I took it back from him and put it away.

'OK,' he said, 'OK.' At least he had stopped talking about taking me back across the border. But then he asked, 'You have gun?'

'No,' I said. 'No gun.'

We came to a petrol station, and he pulled up. On the other side of the pumps was a car with a gang of young lads round it. The driver touched my bag, with all the kit in it. 'What is all this?' he asked.

'Nothing, nothing. Just my things.'

He reached over to pat me on my stomach, to feel if I had a weapon concealed about me.

'No,' I protested. 'I've got nothing.'

Suddenly he called out to the lads by the pump,

and one of them came over. The boy stood by the window. He didn't look at me, but straight at the bag. The driver went on talking to him – until suddenly he ran off into the building.

There's something going on here, I thought. *There's going to be a lynching party coming out. They're going to do me for my weapon, or put me back across the border.*

It was time to go.

I opened the door, grabbed the bag and began to get out. At that moment the driver seized my left arm, trying to hold me back. I dragged him across the front seat and half out of the vehicle. When I kicked the door shut, it caught his head in the opening and he had to let go of me. He let out a yell, and I took off.

Fear boiled up in me again, almost worse than before. Away I went, running up the street, with the plastic sack in one hand. At least, I *thought* I was running – but when I turned round I saw a load of old guys easily keeping up with me. I was running in slow motion. I couldn't go any faster.

Soon there was a big commotion, and a crowd of over a dozen people coming after me. They were barely thirty metres behind me and closing fast.

Somehow, these Syrians knew I had a weapon in that bag. They were out to get it, and then to throw me back into Iraq, or worse. The pavements were full of people, and the ones on the other side of the road were all looking, alerted by the noise. Ahead of me, more pedestrians were staring. I kept hobbling and staggering along, hampered by the plastic sack in my right hand. I couldn't even wave my weapon in threat, because it was stripped down. To put it back together would mean stopping for at least a minute, and by then the mob would have been on top of me.

Then, as I turned a corner, a miracle: there stood a man with an AK-47, wearing chest webbing. He was right next door to a pillar box, obviously on duty. It flashed into my mind that this might be the Iraqi border post, but it was too late to worry.

'Police?' I shouted. 'Police?'

I don't know what the guy said. I'm not sure he said anything at all. He just pulled me through a gateway and into a walled garden. I saw bunting of triangular flags over the entrance, greenery all around, and a big bungalow. He had me by the arm and the scruff of the neck, and ran me into this enclosure, out of reach of the crowd in the street, who by then were yelling for my blood. What his motives were, I'll never know. He may have been trying to save me from the mob, or he may just have thought he'd grabbed a prisoner.

Inside the bungalow a man sat behind a desk, smoking. He was wearing a black leather jacket. So were the other men in there – black leather bomber jackets and jeans – and they all seemed to be smoking. Nobody spoke a word of English. There was a lot of pointing.

'I'm a helicopter pilot,' I said. I started making chopper noises, whirling my hand round to indicate rotors, and then diving it down to show that I had crashed.

Very soon they'd opened my bag and got out the 203, together with my webbing. Then the driver who'd given me the lift rushed in and started shouting in Arabic, jabbing his finger in my direction.

I felt another surge of fear, and motioned to the bomber-jacketed guys. 'Get him out!' I pleaded. They bundled him into another room.

These guys in leather obviously had no time for the driver, but they didn't like the look of me either. I couldn't blame them. My hair was matted with dirt; my face was thin, my eyes staring. I had ten days' growth of beard. I was filthy and stinking. I was also an infidel.

They started stripping my kit, and pulled out the two white phosphorus grenades. One of the guys, who was smoking a cigarette, held a grenade up. 'What's this?' he asked in Arabic.

'Smoke,' I told him. 'For making smoke.' I waved up clouds of the stuff in mid-air.

They started lobbing the grenades round, one to another, catching them like cricket balls. The safety pins, which I'd loosened before our first contact, were hanging out. I knew that if one of the grenades went off, it would kill us all; so I made to stand up and grab them. That didn't go down well. The instant I was half-upright, three guys pulled pistols and levelled them at me, yelling at me to sit down. So I sat back, and everything gradually calmed down. The man who'd finished up with the grenades brought them over, and let me push the pins back into place.

By then the others were ripping out all my kit: the night-sight, my little binoculars. All my stuff was disappearing, and I thought, *I'm not going to see any of this again.* None of it was particularly valuable, but I'd become quite attached to it, having carried it all that way. Now it was being stolen in front of my eyes.

After about twenty minutes I was taken through a door into another room. In came a man of fifty or so, wearing a grey suit. He sat me down at a table with a piece of paper and said, 'Details? Name? Birthday? Country?'

I wrote down: 'Sergeant Chris Ryan, 22 Turbo Squadron, Para Field Ambulance,' followed by my date of birth, and left it at that. 22 Para Field Ambulance didn't exist, but I thought that if I finished up in a prison camp, and the number, combined with the word 'Turbo', reached the Coalition, somebody would click on to the fact that I was a medic in 22 SAS. I gave my rank as sergeant because I knew it would command a bit more respect than if I said 'corporal'.

While I was writing, I was given a cup of coffee. It was thick and bitter, Arab-style, and made me feel thirstier than ever. The man took the paper, went out, then came back in and beckoned me to follow him. Two other guys were waiting outside. They grabbed me by the arms and pulled me into a different room. There they pointed down at a white dishdash and motioned me to put it on.

Now I was really scared. What were they doing, making me dress up like an Arab? The dishdash came down to my feet. Someone then came in with a shamag and wrapped it round my head. At first I could just about see out, but then they pulled it right down over my face.

Nobody told me where I was going or what was happening, and I felt panic rising. I had handed myself over to these people, and they now had complete control of me.

I saw my bag of equipment go out the door ahead of me. A Land Cruiser pulled up outside. Two men armed with AK-47s came in. I was passed over to them and marched out. One man climbed into the driver's seat, I was pushed into the middle, and the second man got in on my right.

As we drove out of the police station, I held my breath. I felt certain that if we turned right, we would be on our way back to Iraq. If we turned left, there was a good chance that the Syrians would be keeping me.

We turned left. I breathed again.

We sped off, along rough streets full of kids playing. The driver didn't stop for them; he just kept going, with one hand on the horn, swerving in and out of the vast potholes. After a while the passenger made signs to ask if I was hungry.

I nodded a yes.

The driver stopped and waited while his mate ran out, returning with a bag of apples. When I ate the whole of the one he gave me – core, pips and all: everything except the stalk – both Arabs stared at me. The one on my right hadn't touched his apple, and he gave it to me. So I ate that too, core and all again.

On we went, missing hundreds of dogs by inches. We swerved to avoid lots of dead ones too. Next we cleared the town, came onto a metalled road and down into a big valley. Then we were out in the desert, on a road that ran straight for miles.

I knew my bag was in the back, but I couldn't tell how much of my kit was still in it. I tried talking, and asked where we were going. 'Damascus?' I suggested. 'Damascus?'

No answer, so I shut up.

After a while, we came to two dark blue Mercedes parked on the side of the road, with a group of six men standing round the cars. As we came towards them, my escorts started talking to each other. Obviously this was some pre-arranged rendezvous. We began to slow down. Fifty metres short of the cars, I could see that one of the waiting men had a pistol in his hand. Suddenly the guy on my right pulled up my shamag, quite roughly, so as to blindfold me, and grabbed hold of my arm.

It's an execution squad, I thought to myself, and my blood ran cold.

We came to a halt. I was dragged out, run up to the back of one of the Mercedes and thrown down on my knees. Somebody pushed my head forward and I sensed someone standing behind me.

Silence.

Nobody moved or spoke.

I thought I was going to die.

Until then I'd always reckoned that if anything like this happened to me, I'd make a last-ditch run for it. But I was physically incapable of running. I just knelt there, waiting for him to shoot me in the back of the head. It was a terrible feeling, to be on my knees, expecting someone to do that to me.

The silence seemed to last for ever. In fact, it was probably less than a minute. Then there was a movement. I was pulled to my feet and thrown into the back of a car. The doors slammed and we drove off again.

Now I had three escorts, all in Western civilian clothes. On my left sat the youngest, a skinny fellow with a thin, weaseley face and a straggling moustache. He struck me as a weak character. The driver was quite a big fellow – dark, good-looking, maybe my own age, and wearing a black leather jacket. His front-seat passenger was about forty: chubby, and going thin on top, he wore a green safari-type jacket with patch pockets. All three had ties, but they had pulled the knots loose, and their appearance was scruffy.

Who were these guys? Police, I hoped. But why were they messing about so much? In my state of exhaustion and confusion, I didn't know what to think. I considered trying to take them out. I still had my knife on me – but the car was travelling fast, probably at 70 or 80 mph for most of the time. Also, there was another car escorting us, and police outriders. The desert we were going through was very open, with nowhere to hide.

My shamag was still on, but the guy in the passenger seat pulled it down far enough for me to see. Then, leaning over into the back, he began to strip-search me: he took off my ID discs by pulling the cord over my head, undid my boot laces, removed my watch, emptied my pockets, took my notebook and map. He missed my belt, which had the gold sovereigns taped to the inside.

That was another frightening moment. *If I'm going to safety*, I thought, *they shouldn't be doing this to me.* Could these fellows really be the Syrian police? If not, who were they? Why were they behaving like this? It was all very strange and alarming.

After a while they blindfolded me again. They talked a bit among themselves, and played loud Arabic music on the stereo. They also chain-smoked.

Soon I was in agony. In the warmth of the car – the highest temperature I'd been in for days – my feet and knees began to swell. The pain became excruciating and I kept trying to ease the agony by shifting around. I was finding it harder and harder to breathe, especially with all the cigarette smoke, and I started feeling claustrophobic. 'Can't you take the blindfold off?' I asked. Until then, whenever I'd tried to pull the shamag off my face, the guy in front had twitched it back. Now, though, he seemed to realize that I was in trouble, and let it drop out of the way.

The second Mercedes was ahead of us now.

Whenever we came to a village, our outriders went ahead on their motorbikes to seal off any side roads, so that we could go speeding straight through. Then they'd come howling past us and take the lead again.

The scrawny fellow next to me kept poking me in the ribs and going on about the war. 'What were you doing in Iraq? You shouldn't be here. Do you like Americans?'

At any other time I'd have thumped him. As it was, I grunted short answers. I didn't want to give anything away. I still didn't know who these people were, or what they were doing. I felt fairly confident they weren't taking me to Baghdad, the capital of Iraq and Saddam Hussein's centre of power, but I thought they might be going to hand me over to some terrorist group as a hostage.

Sometimes our driver would overtake the other car and lead for a while. Every time we came to a village, one of my escorts would pull the shamag over my eyes so that I couldn't see any names. But after four or five hours I looked ahead and saw a motorway sign coming up.

In enormous letters it said: BAGHDAD. With a big arrow pointing from right to left.

My heart dropped.

The driver said something to the fellow beside me, who started poking me in the ribs and cackling. 'Yes, you right. You going Baghdad! You going where Baghdad is.'

I was growing angry – partly with the idiot beside me, partly with myself. How the hell had I ended up in such a situation? Why had I given myself up to these people? Why hadn't I tried to pinch a vehicle and drive myself to Damascus?

The front-seat passenger turned to me and said, 'Yes – we're Baghdadis.'

I tried to get my mind in gear. I had to accept that I was going to a prison camp. I was going to be interrogated. I was going to get a bad kicking, a beating. *Think your thoughts*, I told myself. *Get organized*.

I considered doing a runner, but it was impossible. I was physically exhausted, and wouldn't have gone a hundred metres. *It's no good*,' I told myself. *They'll have you*. Instead, I sat still, trying not to annoy my escorts by fidgeting.

Every part of me was aching: back, shoulders, knees – but worst of all, my feet. Although I'd drunk the water and tea in the barn that morning,

I was desperately in need of both food and more liquid. I had been weakened more than I realized. My mind was so confused that I couldn't remember the simplest details of everyday life.

Through my blindfold I could see and feel that we were heading towards the sun, and that hour by hour the sun was going down. But what did that mean? Did the sun set in the east or in the west? Unable to remember, I tried to think back to what used to happen when I was a kid. Gradually I got it: from my bedroom at home I could see the sun coming up. That was the direction of Newcastle and, further off, China. That meant the sun rose in the east, and set in the west. Now we were heading into the setting sun: therefore we must be driving west.

In that case, I told myself, we *couldn't* be going to Baghdad.

For the final half hour or so they kept my head wrapped up. Then darkness fell, and still we went on driving, until in the end we hit the outskirts of some town or city. By then the blindfold was off again, and I started to see signs saying: DAMAS.

Desperately I tried to visualize the map and remember which part of Syria Damascus was in.

I began daring to hope that we were approaching the Syrian capital, and that my companions had just been winding me up.

My escorts started to smarten themselves up. They put out their cigarettes, turned off the radio, slid their ties tight and straightened their clothes, as if preparing to meet somebody important. All that alarmed me. What were they getting ready for?

Then, on a piece of waste ground, we pulled into the kerb, behind yet another Mercedes. The front passenger got out. His place was taken by a man of maybe fifty; he was well-dressed and balding a little. His dark suit gave him a sombre appearance, but at least he looked cool and calm. The other two characters in my car were obviously in awe of him. As he walked towards us they stopped chattering, and more or less sat to attention, hardly daring to breathe.

The new man closed his door and gave a short order. We moved off towards the city centre. Every now and then he snapped a direction at the driver: 'Left . . . right,' and that was all.

After about five minutes he turned round and asked in English, 'Are you OK?'

'Yep,' I nodded

'Won't be long now.'

Then he picked up all the things they'd taken off me – watch, ID discs, boot laces and so on – and handed them back. 'These are yours,' he said.

I was so confused. What was the point of taking it all off me in the first place? There'd been so many changes of mood.

First the farm boy, definitely friendly.

The driver of the truck had turned hostile, telling me I had no business to be in Syria.

Then the policeman on duty had saved me from the mob.

Next the guys inside the station had tried to steal all my kit.

Then the guy who made me write down my details seemed to be back on my side.

A few minutes later my escorts were giving me apples to eat.

Then it was into the mock-execution, and more sick jokes about going to Baghdad.

No wonder my head was swimming.

I started getting my kit back in place. I put away the maps and knife, and got the ID discs back round my neck. By then my feet had swollen up so much that I couldn't get my boots on, so I didn't bother threading the laces.

At last we came to a big modern building, probably ten storeys high. There were guards in green uniforms and armed with AK-47s on the gates, on the walls, everywhere. It wasn't the sort of place you could break into, or out of, in a hurry. Before I had time to wonder where we were, the gates swung open in front of us, and we drove into a courtyard.

CHAPTER 14
THE SECRET POLICE

All my escorts got out. When I tried to move, I found that my knees and ankles had locked solid. The older guy saw me struggling and clicked his fingers. The other two lifted me out of the car and practically carried me up a long flight of steps to the glass doors. They can't have enjoyed it much, because I absolutely stank.

After a few steps my legs began to function again, more or less. We shuffled into a big reception area, where everything looked efficient and well-guarded. We got into a lift and went up a few floors. As the doors opened, we were met by a smartly dressed, clean-shaven man in a dark blue blazer, stripey tie and blue shirt. Beside him, hovering respectfully, stood another man, about the same age, but chubbier and less smart.

The boss-figure in the stripey tie was an impressive character: in his mid-forties, he had a good haircut and possessed obvious authority. I hadn't a clue who he was and he didn't tell me. Only later did I discover that he was head of the Mukhabarat, the Syrian Secret Police.

The boss smiled, reached out, took my hand, and said in English, 'Welcome to Damascus. Welcome to Syria.'

The chubby man, who was an interpreter, said, 'Come in, please.' He ushered me in.

Where was the catch? What were they up to? I was desperately trying to think through all my options – and think fast – so that I didn't get caught out.

I followed them through into some kind of office and sat down on a sofa. I could see the boss sniff, not liking the smell of me. Now that I was somewhere clean, I could see what a terrible state I was in: my hair was matted, my hands and face were filthy. There was brown, dried blood on my DPMs. The boss himself took off the shamag, which was still wrapped round my head. He spoke sharply to the interpreter, clearly saying, 'Get this stuff off.' Someone else helped me out of the dishdash. Another guy brought in my bag and put it under a table.

'Would you like to get cleaned up?' the boss asked through the interpreter.

'Yeah,' I said. 'Good idea.'

'Come with me.'

The interpreter's English was first class, and he seemed very friendly. I tried to appear grateful; but I still had no idea what was going on, and I expect I looked shell-shocked. I had time to glance round the walls and noticed a gold-plated AK-47, as well as pictures of Hafez al-Assad, the Syrian President. A large, leather-topped desk stood in one corner, covered in ornaments and paperweights. Two or three settees were set out around a coffee table. The whole room spoke of money and good organization.

We walked out of the office, through a living room and into a bedroom, where some exercise machines were set out. Then we went into the bathroom, which had a big corner bath, a shower, a toilet, a pedestal basin with a mirror on the wall above it, and shelves full of toiletries. Everything was clean and glitzy, with gold-plated taps.

The boss walked around, fitting a new blade into a safety razor and getting some shampoo ready. Someone turned on the bath, and through the interpreter he said, 'This is all my stuff. Just use it, please.'

He went out and left me alone. It was only then that I looked in a mirror and saw my face. What a sight! I was gaunt as a skeleton; under ten days' growth of beard my cheeks were hollow, and my eyes seemed to have sunk into their sockets. My hair was matted with every kind of filth.

I felt stunned, unable to make out what was happening. One minute I'd been gearing myself up for prison; now I was being taken care of in a high-class apartment. But whatever else lay ahead, there was no reason not to have a bath. I started slowly undressing, and took off my shirt.

Looking in two mirrors at once (one in front, one behind), I caught sight of my back, and I could hardly believe it. My ribs, spine and hipbones were all sticking out, as though I'd been starved for weeks. I could see every rib going round and joining my backbone. It was a shock to realize that I'd been living off my own body. In walking nearly 300 kilometres, and shuddering with cold for countless hours, I'd burned away all the muscle which I'd built up during my time on the SP team.

In the mirror I saw a young boy coming in holding a tape measure, and the interpreter behind him.

'What's going on now?' I demanded.

'We'll just take your sizes,' said the interpreter, and the boy started measuring me.

What's this for? I was thinking. *A coffin?* But I didn't ask – partly out of fear that I would learn something bad.

The boy soon legged it, and as I was getting my trousers off, in came another guy with a cup of Turkish coffee. I drank a mouthful of it, but it tasted like cough medicine and made me gag. 'Water!' I croaked, and made drinking motions.

I edged myself over the bath and lowered myself in carefully, backside first, keeping my feet out of the water. Then I gradually submerged them. As the heat hit the cuts, the pain was horrendous. After a few seconds I lifted them out again, then tried to lower them back into the water. I lay there with my legs up as I washed myself and shampooed my hair. Soon the water was absolutely black, so I got out, pulled out the plug, and started to fill the bath again.

I got back into clean water, and again the pain in my feet was terrific, as if needles were being driven into them. Apart from the cuts along the sides, they were discoloured, with red and blue patches. All I could do was lie there and bite my tongue. After a while the burning ache subsided, and I started to enjoy the hot water.

The interpreter came in and sat down by the bath with his notepad. 'Right,' he said. 'Can you tell me what happened?'

Play it like you're frightened, I thought. 'I'm a medic,' I told him. 'I was brought in from the TA, and I was on board a helicopter going in to retrieve—'

'The TA?'

'The Territorial Army. The reserves. As I said, I was going in to retrieve a downed pilot, and something happened. There was a big bang, the helicopter crashed, and I just ran for it. We came down, and I was really scared. I didn't wait for anybody else . . .' *Keep it light*, I was thinking. *Pretend to be nervous.*

'How long ago?'

'Three days, I think.'

'Whereabouts was the crash?'

'I don't know. I just ran. I had no idea where we were.'

'What sort of helicopter was it?'

'A Sea King.'

'What did it look like?'

'Just a helicopter . . . Single engine.'

The interpreter had been watching me closely. 'OK,' he said, and left the room. I didn't think he'd believed a word I'd said. Too bad. I climbed out of the bath and got my beard off with a couple of shaves. Without the stubble, I looked very thin and tired. My lips were cracked and broken, but no more than if I'd been in the sun too long.

As I was drying myself, the boy who'd measured me brought in a set of clean white underpants and vest and laid them on the toilet seat. Also, he picked up my own stinking kit, and took it out.

Spotting a pair of scales, I stood on them. At first I thought the needle had jammed, so I shook the platform about but it stayed steady on 63.5 kg, or 140 lb. Ten days earlier I'd been 80 kg, or 176 lb. I'd lost 36 lb – over 16 kg.

I pulled on the clean underwear and walked out into the bedroom. Waiting for me was a brand-new blue corduroy suit, together with a white shirt and a tie. By then it was eleven o'clock at night. The secret police must have told a tailor to put the suit together in half an hour. They clearly had influence. There was also a pair of black slip-on shoes.

As I started to get dressed, the boss noticed the state of my feet. He telephoned for a medical orderly, while I sat on the edge of the bed and waited. Soon a medic appeared. He cleaned out the cuts with a lotion that stung, and put plasters on, but he made such a mess of the job that I reckoned I could have done better on my own. If they'd had any zinc oxide tape, I'd have taped my feet right up. Also, I knew I needed some antibiotics. By then my ankles as well as my feet were swollen, and the new pair of shoes wouldn't go on. I stayed in my socks.

Suddenly a horrible thought hit me. *It's a press conference. They're dressing me up for a staged press do. I'm going to walk into a room full of lights and reporters and cameramen. They'll all be asking questions. What am I going to tell them?*

I hadn't a clue what was happening in Iraq. I presumed that the air war was still going on – but I didn't know if the ground war had started. I didn't even know what had become of the rest of my patrol.

If I said the wrong thing now, I could blow the whole SAS operation in the Gulf.

I could blow the fact that the Regiment was in Saudi.

Did the Syrians realize I was in the SAS?

Maybe I should tell them the truth, in the hope that they'd keep it quiet. One way or another, I could be in big trouble.

Before I had time to worry too much, they moved me back into the sitting room and the boss told the interpreter to switch on the TV. He tuned to CNN, and I soon saw that the air war *was* still on – Allied aircraft were bombing Baghdad – but there appeared to have been no major action on the ground.

'Are you hungry?' the interpreter asked me.

Hungry? In the past eight days I'd eaten two packets of biscuits and two apples. 'Yes,' I said. 'I am.'

'Just a minute, then.'

He let me watch CNN for a while, then led me through to the other lounge. My feet felt quite easy on the carpet, but I was sore and stiff all over. In my brief absence someone had set out a feast on a table. There were kebabs, steaks, rice, salads, bread and fruit.

'You must be starving,' the interpreter said. He heaped a pile of food onto my plate. The smell was fantastic, but when I cut into a steak and took one bite of it, it seemed to stick in my throat and I couldn't eat any more.

I just sat there drinking pints of water. 'Is the food bad?' asked the boss.

'No,' I said. 'It's just that I'm not as hungry as I thought. More thirsty. I'm sorry.'

The other two had been eating, but I got the impression they were only doing it to be polite. As soon as I gave up, they did too. Back in the other room, the interpreter asked, 'Well, what would you like to do now? How about seeing some Syrian nightlife?'

What? I was astounded. Didn't these guys realize what a state I was in?

'No thanks,' I muttered. 'I can't walk.'

'Well, do you need anything?'

'Can you take me to the British Embassy?'

'Oh? You want to go there?' He seemed rather surprised.

'Yes, if it's possible.'

'OK.' He began making phone calls. While he was doing that, I was led across to a table – and there was all my kit which had been taken away in the police station, and which I thought had been stolen.

'Well,' said the interpreter, coming over, 'is everything there?'

I made a check, and found everything present – weapon, ammunition, night-sight, even the white phos grenades.

'Yeah,' I said. 'It's all there.'

'This is interesting.' He picked up the night-sight. 'What's this?'

'Oh, just a thing they gave us so that we could see in the dark.' I felt sure he knew what it was, so I showed him how to turn it on, and he stood there looking out of the window with it, down into the courtyard.

'Brilliant!' he said. 'I'll have everything packed away for you.'

I think they knew exactly who I was, but they were playing along with my story.

'You know,' said the interpreter keenly, 'I've always wanted to come to England for a holiday. Where do you live?'

'In Newcastle,' I said. 'With my parents.'

'Oh, I'd love to come there. Can you give me your

telephone number and address? Maybe you could show us the sights and return our hospitality some time? Could I give you a ring?'

I made up a number, giving the Rowlands Gill code with changed digits, and a phoney address.

'By the way,' the interpreter added as we were waiting. 'Did you see anyone as you crossed the border? Did anyone meet you?'

That made me think they must have had people out on their own side of the frontier, watching, and waiting to receive escapees. 'No,' I told him. 'I didn't see anybody.'

'So you found the police station yourself?'

'That's right.' I told them more or less what had happened at the farmhouse.

'And this young boy who took you in – where was his house?'

I tried to describe the location, and the boss promised to send someone to thank the people there. 'How was your journey after that?' he asked.

I thought, *If I tell him about the fake execution and everything else that happened in the desert, he may keep me here for days, until he's had the guys dragged in.*

'Oh, it was fine, thanks,' I said. 'No problem.'

There was a knock at the door, and in came the driver of the car. He was actually cowering, dry-washing his hands in front of him, with his head hanging down. *Who is this boss guy?* I wondered. *What does he do to people to make them behave like that?*

The interpreter gave me a piece of paper with a telephone number on it, and said, 'If you have any problems in Damascus, ring this number and ask to speak to me.' I put the note in my pocket and tucked my new shoes under one arm. Then I shook hands with the boss, who patted me on the back. 'The car will take you to the British Embassy,' he said, 'and staff of the embassy will meet you there.'

I limped downstairs and found a Mercedes waiting. In we climbed, and the driver set off.

CHAPTER 15
FRIENDS IN HIGH PLACES

The embassy was a disappointment. It turned out to be a boring office building, although there were a lot of guards dotted all over the place in ones and twos with weapons. As we pulled up, I grabbed my bag, thanked the driver and got out. It was a little before 1 a.m.

A young man was standing on the steps, waiting to meet me. He introduced himself as the second secretary, and I soon saw that he was a switched-on lad – tall, dark-haired, wearing glasses, in his early thirties, and quite smart looking. With him was the defence attaché – older, clearly an officer of sorts, fortyish, short, dark-haired as well.

'Who are you?' he asked.

'Sergeant Ryan from 22 SAS.'

'OK. Upstairs.'

I dragged myself up one flight and sat down in a room. What with the state of my hands, and blood oozing out of my stockinged feet, you might have thought the DA would give me an easy time. Not at all.

'Right,' he said, 'I'm just going to ask you a few questions, to verify who you are – make sure you're not a plant. What's your parent unit? Who's the commanding officer?'

I stared at the guy. 'Listen,' I said. 'Don't start. I'm from 22 SAS, and I've been on the run for eight days. Just get a message back to High Wycombe.'

That woke him up. He gave a kind of choke. 'Look, cool it,' the second secretary told him. The DA seemed to have no inkling of what had been going on behind the scenes in Iraq, but I got the impression that the second secretary had a pretty good idea.

'There's nobody else come out, then?' I asked.

The DA stared at me. 'No, you're the first we've seen.'

'Can you tell us what happened?' the second secretary asked.

So I gave them a broad outline of the story: how

the patrol had been deployed and had a contact, how we'd legged it through the desert, split up, lost Vince, moved on, had another contact, and so on.

The DA seemed amazed that anyone should have walked out into Syria. 'Nobody told us you were anywhere near the border,' he said. But then he let on that, a few days before, he'd had a visit from two British guys doing some sort of a recce. When I heard their names, I realized they were from the Regiment, and that they'd been making a security assessment. After I said I knew both of them, things began to make more sense to him. He warned me that the building was probably bugged, which meant the Syrians could be listening to every word we said. I just hoped they'd packed up for the night. Otherwise they'd immediately know that I'd been lying an hour or two earlier.

The DA wrote down some details of what I'd told him and brought in one of the communications clerks, a girl, who encoded a message and sent it off to the UK command centre at High Wycombe.

Once the message was sent, I reassembled my weapon and secured it, together with my ammunition, grenades, TACBE and night-sight, in the strong room. Then they told me that I could spend the rest of the night in the Meridien Hotel, just down the road. They felt that the hotel would be secure enough, but they told me to stay in my room and to order meals through room service. They said they'd put me on the British Airways flight to London the next day.

London! That wasn't what I wanted at all. My only concern was to get back to Saudi and find out what had become of the rest of the patrol. But I realized that if I did fly in to London, I'd only have a very short time there – the Regiment would want me straight back in Saudi, for debriefing.

The embassy guys offered to get a taxi down to the hotel, but as it was only a couple of hundred metres away, I said I could walk. Yet when the DA set off at a normal pace, I couldn't keep up with him. I padded slowly along the pavement, and anyone I passed looked down at my stockinged feet in some surprise. As we arrived at the hotel, the porters standing around in the lobby also glared at my feet.

'We may have a bit of trouble here,' the second secretary said, 'as you haven't got a passport.

They don't normally let anybody book in without identification. But I'll see if I can square it away.'

Sure enough, the guy on the desk wasn't amused. 'No, no,' he kept saying. 'No passport, no room! He cannot book in.'

The second secretary began muttering about going back to the embassy and spending the night there. He said that to get a passport made out he'd have to contact the chargé d'affaires. A photo would have to be taken, and it couldn't be done until next morning.

'Listen,' I said. 'I've got a telephone number from the police. The boss guy said if I had any trouble, I was to ring them.'

'No, no,' said the defence attaché hurriedly. 'You can't do that. Don't ring them. Don't involve them any more. In fact, we've got a cellar bedroom in the embassy, and you can sleep down there.'

'No,' said the second secretary. 'The place is filthy. He can't go in there.'

'Nonsense!' barked the DA. 'He's just roughed it for eight days. He'll be all right.' Then he added, 'At a pinch, he can have my bed.'

We didn't seem to be getting far, so the second secretary said, 'Where's that telephone number?'

He got on the phone to my friend in the secret police, and within five minutes two Mercedes screeched to a halt outside. A swarm of men ran in. It looked like a raid by the SS in a Second World War film; some of them were wearing long black leather trench coats.

With them was the interpreter. He came running up to me, grabbed me by the arm and moved me to one side. 'Chris,' he said quietly. 'In two minutes, you're going to sign the book. Sign with a name that you can remember, and give any address you can remember. Everything will be all right. If you get any more trouble, ring me again.' He then had a word with the second secretary.

I turned round, and there were three blokes giving the hotel manager behind the desk a hard time. His eyes were going round in circles, and he was nodding like a robot.

'I'll see you later,' said the interpreter, and then the secret police party walked out.

I went back up to the desk.

'Yes, yes. Sign here, please. Anything I can do for you, sir?'

I gave my surname as Black, and made up some address near Newcastle. The man snapped his fingers for a porter, and two guys grabbed my bags. The diplomats said, 'We'll see you in the morning,' and up I went.

By then it was after 2 a.m. and the past twenty-four hours had been the longest of my life. I'd really been looking forward to getting into that room. *Once I close the door*, I thought, *I'll be free of worry and danger for the first time in ten days. I'll be able to lie down, chill out, and go to sleep.*

But it didn't work out like that. As soon as I was alone, I started worrying about the rest of the patrol. I'd hoped that some of the guys would have escaped into Syria ahead of me. Either that, or they would have been lifted out by chopper, back into Saudi; but now these possibilities seemed unlikely. If the five had been rescued, and three guys had still been missing, the Regiment would surely have alerted the Syrians to look out for us, and warned the Damascus embassy. I'd come up like a bad penny, but nobody else had. What had happened to the others? Were they dead, or hiding up somewhere? Were they still on the move? If they were, they must be in a bad way by now.

I was so wound up that I felt I was still on the

run. I got out my notebook and began scribbling reminders about what I'd done. I'd brought the book with me in case I had to take down a radio message or compose one. Until then, I hadn't made a single entry, for fear that I might be captured. But now I went back one day at a time, logging details to refresh my memory, and working out where I'd been at various times.

At last I got my head down. But still I was tossing and turning, my mind full of disturbing images – of my comrades wandering in the desert, or worse still being killed.

In the end, though, I fell asleep – only to be dragged back by the phone ringing just after 3 a.m. It was the defence attaché on the line, speaking in hushed whispers.

'What happened to the Charlie Oscar Delta Echo Sierra?' he breathed.

'What?'

He repeated himself.

'What are you on about?'

'What happened to the *codes*?'

Suddenly I realized that he was trying to be covert, spelling out 'codes' like that. Also I realized that it must be High Wycombe who were asking for the information. Whenever we encrypt a message, we put it into code, then burn the cipher and smash the encryption device. In fact, Legs had carried our cipher equipment. He had burned the codes and smashed the device when we were first compromised.

'One of the other lads had them,' I said. 'He burned them. I never had them at all.'

'OK,' he said, and rang off.

That was when I knew for sure that nobody else had come out.

In the morning I ordered breakfast from room service, and ate some fruit salad and a roll. I still didn't want anything substantial, but I drank pints of fruit juice and tea. Compared with the day before, I felt quite good. Then the Brits came to collect me, and I hobbled back to the embassy, shuffling along the pavement in my stockinged feet, with my shoes under my arm.

By the time we arrived, the place was full of people. The chargé d'affaires had appeared, and there were two British girls on duty, one dealing with communications, the other a typist. I chatted to them for a while, then they put me up against a wall in my shirt and tie to take a black-and-white passport photograph with a Polaroid camera. 'Better be careful,' somebody said. 'We've only got two frames left.' But the first shot came out well, so they trimmed it, stuck it into a blank passport and stamped it. There I was, fixed up with a ten-year passport. The whole thing seemed so amateurish that I felt I was being given a Second World War escape kit.

During the morning some questions came back from High Wycombe. I mentioned that I'd walked through some installation which looked like a signals complex.

'No,' the second secretary said. 'That's not a signals complex. That's the yellowcake processing facility at Al Qaim.' He knew everything about the place – even the number of the Iraqi regiment guarding it. The latticework towers I'd seen on the high ground were for defence, not communication: the cables slung between them were in fact chains, to prevent attacks from low-flying aircraft.

'What's going on there?' I asked.

'We don't know exactly. Some sort of nuclear processing.'

'*What?* I drank some water coming out of that place, and it tasted terrible.'

'Effluent,' he said. 'Nuclear effluent.'

I felt my insides go cold. Had I swallowed some radioactive waste and contaminated myself, maybe with fatal consequences?

Later we headed down to the airport to buy a ticket and get me on the flight to London. I got as far as the check-in desk, but there the guy stopped me because I didn't have a stamped visa showing when I'd entered the country. I couldn't argue with him, and I ended up back at the embassy. It looked like I'd have to stay in Syria for a couple of days.

I went off with the defence attaché to see about a visa. We visited a building which was full of tiny offices. We were passed from pillar to post. All in all we saw about twenty people. 'Well,' the final official said, 'if you haven't got an entry visa, you can't leave.'

So we'd wasted the whole morning. I said to the DA, 'Why not phone my friend in the police again?'

'Oh no,' he said, 'we can't do that.'

So I waited till I was away from him, and asked the second secretary the same question. He put through a call, and very soon a message was on its way from the police to the visa building. When we next went down, I collected my exit visa without difficulty.

The next flight out was in two days' time – but now things had changed. Instead of returning to the UK, I was told I'd be flying to Cyprus, where I'd be put onto a Hercules that was coming across from Riyadh, the capital of Saudi Arabia. From Cyprus I was to fly to the Saudi capital, spend one night there, and then return to the squadron at Al Jouf. That suited me much better. All I wanted was to get back to the squadron, so that I could find out about the rest of the patrol, and brief any other guys who might be going in.

That evening, back in the hotel, I had a meal in my room and went to bed. But still I couldn't relax: the missing guys were too much on my mind. It felt really bad to be sitting in Damascus, unable to contribute any information which might help with their recovery.

Back in the embassy next day, I was chatting to the two girls. One of them suggested I'd be more comfortable chilling out in her flat. As we sat there talking, I said, 'D'you mind if I take off my shoes and socks, and have another look at my feet?'

By then the cuts had dried up a good bit, but they still weren't a pretty sight, and when I stripped the dressings off, they were horrified. Until then, I don't think either of the girls quite realized what I'd been through. They imagined I'd just been for a bit of a walk. Anyway, they were full of sympathy – and it was good just to sit there and let my feet breathe.

My fingers were nearly as bad as my feet. I still had no feeling in the tips, and when I squeezed my nails, pus kept oozing out. So I asked if she'd got a scrubbing brush, and went to the basin and scrubbed my fingers really hard. It was total agony, but I got the dirt out from under the nails, and all the pus, until blood was running freely. Then I rinsed my hands off. I hoped they would now begin to heal. Obviously I should have seen a doctor, but the embassy had no medic in residence, and a message from High Wycombe had told me not to make contact with anyone outside.

The embassy people did their best to entertain me. The DA's assistant, a sergeant, took me out for a drive round the heights of Damascus and showed me some of the military installations. We chatted about my escape. 'You're going to get a medal for this,' he said.

'Why?' I asked. 'It was nothing special.'

Until that moment it hadn't occurred to me that I'd done anything exceptional. I'd just been for rather a long walk. The job we'd been tasked to do had proved rather more difficult than expected – but I'd had to go through with it all the same.

When the time came to leave, my weapon and ammunition obviously had to stay behind, but I wanted to take the TACBE and the night-sight, because I knew that those things were in short supply back at the squadron. But the second secretary made me leave them, in case they aroused suspicion and got me pulled in for questioning at the airport.

When I went to board the Syrian Airlines aircraft I kept my bag with me, but as I reached the top of the steps, the steward said something aggressive to me in Arabic and threw it back down to the ground. As I went in through the door, I could only hope that someone would put it on board. On the plane, my seat was right at the back. As soon as we were airborne, with the no-smoking lights still on, everyone lit cigarettes. I've never been on an aircraft so full of smoke; you couldn't see from one end of the cabin to the other.

I didn't care about any of that. I was just relieved

to be leaving Syria. Even in the hands of the embassy people, I'd never felt entirely safe. Damascus had a dangerous air about it, and memories of the mock-execution out in the desert kept me on edge.

It seemed crazy to be flying to Cyprus. The island lies more or less due west of Damascus, and it was east that I wanted to be heading. But the flight lasted less than a couple of hours, and soon we were coming in to land at Larnaca.

All the while I had only one thing on my mind: what was the score back in the squadron?

CHAPTER 16
BACK TO BASE

The defence attaché had arranged for me to be met in Cyprus, and once I'd collected my bag – which I was relieved to see had got on board OK – and got it through customs, I was met by a guy from the Joint Intelligence Company. He didn't know who I was – just that I was passing through. As he led me across to a car, he said he was taking me to a family who'd agreed to put me up. Once we were rolling, he asked if I needed to see anybody.

'Yes,' I said. 'I need to see a doctor.'

'What's wrong?'

'Well, for starters, I think I drank some poisonous water. Also, my feet are in bits. And look at that.'

I held out my hand to show him my fingers, which had not only lost all feeling in the tips, but now seemed to be turning blue. He gave me a strange look, but I didn't tell him where I'd been.

We drove into a nice-looking housing estate, with guards on the entrance, and I was met by an RAF squadron leader, who introduced me to his Scottish wife and their two young kids. No questions were asked; obviously they'd been briefed. They just welcomed me and sat me down.

'Can I make you something to eat for tea?' the wife asked. 'It won't take a minute. *EastEnders* is on the telly.'

So there I sat, watching *EastEnders* and eating eggs, beans and chips. After everything I'd been through, it felt really weird.

A doctor turned up and asked me what was wrong.

'It's my fingers,' I told him. 'I can't feel them much, and they keep going blue.'

He did the squeeze test a few times and said, 'Well, the colour seems to be coming back. I think you've got a bit of frost-nip, that's all.' Then he looked at my feet, cleaned them up as much as he could, put zinc oxide tape on them and left me some spare tape. 'There's not a lot I can do for you,' he said. 'Is there anything else wrong?'

'Well, I was round a chemical plant and drank some of the effluent. Could that be having an effect on my hands?'

'I don't see how it could. But you ought to have blood tests and other checks when you get back home.'

When he'd gone, the woman gave me a beer, which went down well, and we sat around chatting. Then, just before 8 p.m., the husband said, 'Right, I'm off to work. I'll be back at four in the morning to pick you up.'

My hostess showed me to a bedroom. 'Would you like to get your head down?' she asked.

'Great,' I said. But first I went to have a bath, because I'd got so sticky on the aircraft. When I stripped off, I was shocked. My legs had gone blue – worse than my hands!

For a few seconds I was horrified – then I realized what the problem was. The dye had been coming out of my new Syrian cords, onto my hands as well. What a wally I felt, after that scene with the doctor! At least now I knew why I kept turning blue. But no matter what their colour was, my hands weren't right; my fingers were still feeling woody.

I got my head down, and the next thing I knew,

my host was knocking on my door at 4 a.m. His wife was already up and had made a cup of tea; she was waiting for us downstairs, and as we went out I thanked her for looking after me.

At Akrotiri airbase we were confronted by an RAF corporal. 'Where's your ID card?' he demanded.

'I haven't got one.'

'Passport?'

'Haven't got one.' (In fact, I had the passport which they'd made out for me in Damascus, but I wasn't going to show it to him.)

'Name?'

'There's no name.'

'Well, who are you?'

'I'm a person that's getting on this flight.'

Behind me was the squadron leader who'd been looking after me. He was carrying my bags, and now he said, 'It's all right. I'll vouch for him.'

'OK, sir,' said the corporal, and we walked through.

By then the flight crew had assembled, and the chief loadie – the flight sergeant in charge of the back of the Hercules – had heard all this. He was quite a big lad, and he stood there watching.

The squadron leader came in, put my bags down

and said, 'You'll be going aboard with this flight crew. Soon as they go, you get on too.' He went across to them and said, 'That's some extra luggage you've got.' Then he shook hands with me. I thanked him, and he left.

The flight crew were all laughing and joking together. I sat by myself across the room, and after a few minutes the flight sergeant came across. 'Who are you, then?' he asked.

'I'm not telling you.'

'What?'

'Mind your own business,' I said, and looked down.

'Who d'you think you are?'

'What's it got to do with you?'

'If you don't tell me who you are,' said the flight sergeant, 'you're not getting on my aircraft.'

'If I don't get on,' I told him, 'I guarantee your career will end when this aircraft touches down in Riyadh. Now stop asking questions.'

It was out of character for me to be so aggressive, but I felt I'd been through so much that I wasn't going to bow down to anybody. These arguments were typical of what happens if someone tries to push an SAS guy. It's a privilege, a sort of power for people in the Regiment – they don't have to tell outsiders anything. With officers, obviously, you're polite, and if they ask for your identity, you just say, 'Sorry, sir, I can't tell you.' Most people have the sense to back off if you tell them in a civil way that they don't need to know. But there are always one or two who push and push, until it comes to the point when you have to lay down the law.

The back of the Herc was packed full of equipment, netted and strapped down on pallets. As I sat on one of the web seats, the first person I saw was Mel, a young signaller from 22 SAS. The flight sergeant knew where Mel came from – so when he saw us together, he realized that I was SAS and that he'd put his foot in it. I tried to find out from Mel if there was any news of the rest of the patrol. There was none.

Four hours later I landed in Riyadh for the second time. I was put up in a hotel, where the Director – the brigadier in command of Special Forces – came to visit me. He was a 'B' Squadron man himself, and he saw my escape as a feather in the squadron's cap. First thing next morning, he said, I was to fly up to Al Jouf on a Hercules. And that was what I'd been waiting for.

* * *

I couldn't come to terms with the fact that there was no news of the others. Because the Iraqis had not announced the capture of any prisoners behind the lines, it seemed more and more likely that they were all dead. Everyone kept asking me what had happened, but the truth was that I wanted to know the score as much as them.

In the morning I dressed in my clean uniform, which had been through the washing machine at the embassy in Damascus. It felt good to have it on again. My feet were still pretty sore, but I got my boots back on, and so looked quite presentable.

As the aircraft landed at Al Jouf I was so excited by the thought of seeing the guys again that I went and stood on the tailgate as it was dropping down, ready to rush out and greet them. But to my surprise there was only one man there – Geordie, the Squadron Sergeant Major. He had told everyone else to keep away, in case I was overwhelmed by emotion. In fact, three of the guys had ignored his instructions and were hovering in the background. As I walked out, they came racing across and surrounded me, hammering me on the back, and calling out, 'Well done!'

For a minute or two I couldn't really speak. One of the guys was so shattered by my appearance that he burst into tears. In place of the fit, bouncing young fellow he'd seen off a couple of weeks earlier, here was a prematurely aged cripple, broken, bent and shuffling. He said I looked like a bag of bones.

Geordie thinned the guys out and took me to one side. 'Right,' he said. 'We've got to go into headquarters for the debriefing.'

The HQ was housed in tents next to the permanent control-tower buildings. Before we went in, Geordie asked if there was anything I wanted to tell him first. I said, 'Yeah, there's quite a bit. I'll tell you what actually happened, but I'm not going to mention it all in the debrief.' So I told him about Vince losing heart. 'If Andy or any of the others come out, they'll confirm it,' I said. 'Until then, we'll just leave it.'

'Fine,' Geordie said, and we went in.

The debrief lasted two hours. Once it was over, Geordie drove me round the airfield to the squadron location. On the way he asked, 'First things first: d'you want to go home?'

'No,' I said. 'I want to stay here and find out

what's happened.' The last thing I wanted to do was desert the team.

It was then that Geordie told me what had happened to the other two Bravo patrols: they'd both come straight back.

When Bravo Three Zero took stock of their location, the commander immediately decided that the area was impossibly dangerous. There wasn't enough cover to conceal the vehicles, so they immediately began to drive back towards the Saudi border – a journey which took them two nights. Afterwards the commander was fiercely criticized, not least because he ignored an instruction to RV with 'D' Squadron – who were already in Iraq and needing reinforcement – not far off his route.

Bravo One Zero stayed an even shorter time. When the Chinook landed at their drop-off point, the pilot said to the leader, 'Pete – d'you want to have a look around while I hang on a minute? I can't see any depressions or wadis for miles. It's like a billiard table.' To prove his point, the pilot flew twenty kilometres up and down, trying to find some broken ground into which he could drop the patrol, but the desert remained horribly bare.

Pete took a decision which struck me as very brave. 'Right,' he said. 'We're not staying here. We're flying out.'

Back at Al Jouf people said he was a coward. But I and many others reckoned that of all the decisions taken by the three patrol commanders, his needed the most courage. A year later people would start to say: 'Well, maybe he did the right thing after all' – but at the time he suffered.

It was a big surprise for me to hear that none of the three planned OPs (observation posts) had therefore been set up.

Bravo Two Zero's comms failure had been due mainly to the fact that we'd been given the wrong radio frequencies. This was not the fault of anyone in the Regiment, but of the signals unit attached to us. The result was that although three of Legs' messages got through in garbled form, no reply ever reached us.

I also found that our TACBEs didn't perform the way we'd been told. Their effective range was only about 120 kilometres, and there were no Coalition aircraft within 500 kilometres to the east. During the night of 24 January – our first on the run – one American F-15 pilot had picked up a call from

Andy, and he passed it on. But because the call came from a location our HQ was not expecting, it only caused confusion.

When the patrol went missing, the guys in the squadron wanted to mount a rescue mission. When the CO refused to commit one of his few precious helicopters immediately to the task, some of the guys were on the verge of mutiny. But in the circumstances middle and senior management agreed that the CO was right to delay a search until the patrol's situation became clearer.

The main problem was that HQ was expecting us to strike back for the Saudi border if in trouble.

But we had set off in exactly the opposite direction.

By 26 January it was clear that something had gone seriously wrong so action was taken. At 1745 that evening a Chinook took off from Arar, with five members of the squadron on board, in an attempt to pull us out. That mission was aborted when the weather got bad.

The next day, a team went in on board an MH-53 helicopter. It flew within five or six kilometres of our original emergency rendezvous point before flying down the most likely escape-and-evasion route to the Saudi border, and almost running out of fuel in the process.

A third search-and-rescue mission was mounted on 30 January, but this was also aborted when the pilot fell ill. The CO continued trying to arrange further searches until, in the early hours of 1 February, he heard that I had turned up in Damascus. It was obvious then that none of the patrol could still be trying to return to Saudi.

More cheerful news was that 'A' and 'D' Squadrons had crossed the border in force just one night after our insertion, and were creating havoc among mobile Scud launchers and communications towers. Their key weapon was the M19 – in effect, a machine gun firing bombs at the rate of three or four per second. The ammunition was the same as in our 203s, except that the rounds contained more high-explosive. When volleys of those things began bursting all around them, the Iraqis turned and ran.

At 2300 the CO said he wanted to see me. I went to one of the control rooms, and was there until two in the morning, being debriefed for a second time. At the end he asked, 'Is there anything you think you should have done?'

That nearly cracked me up: I almost burst into tears as I said, 'I should have tied Vince to me.'

'Listen,' said the CO. 'It wasn't your fault.'

Then he asked if I'd mind going up to Arar, to talk to 'A' Squadron of Delta Force, the American Special Forces unit, which was about to deploy behind the lines. It meant leaving at 0530 – in about three hours' time – so I went straight back to my tent and got my head down. As I climbed into my sleeping bag, the CO draped a big goatherd's coat over me. I felt like a little kid.

Apart from my night in Cyprus, that was the first time since the contact that I slept soundly. I don't know whether it was because I felt secure at last, but the next thing I knew, Geordie was shaking my shoulder. He'd already cooked a fried breakfast with the light on, but I'd been out for the count and hadn't noticed a thing. So we had sausages and bacon and a cup of tea, and set out at 0530 in a Land Rover, accompanied by Gus, an American liaison officer.

All the way up, as it got lighter, Gus was picking information out of me. We'd met before, in

Hereford when he'd come to the UK to command one of the squadrons. (At that time I was Sniper Team Commander, in charge of all the high-rise options – climbing and abseiling on the outsides of buildings, inside lift-wells, or ascending glass buildings on suckers.) Delta's target was the area around the nuclear refinery, and whenever we came to a new kind of terrain during our drive, he asked if the ground where they were heading resembled what we could see. I found I was able to describe the different areas well.

The journey took nearly three hours. Then, in the control room at Arar, I met Major General Wayne Downing, Commander of US Special Forces, who'd recently flown in to supervise operations. Slim, fit-looking, with a crew-cut, he looked just like you'd imagine a successful American soldier to look. He shook my hand and introduced me to four or five other officers. We sat down on sofas round a coffee table, Downing thanked me for coming up, and I told them what had happened. When I finished, there was silence.

'That's the most amazing story I've heard in years,' Downing said. There was a pause, and he asked, 'What have the doctors said?'

'Well – I haven't seen a proper doctor yet.'

He seemed shocked. 'I sure am sorry to have dragged you up here,' he said, looking worried and a bit embarrassed. 'You ought to have seen a doctor before you came. Tell you what, though: we've got some go-faster surgeons on the base. I'll have one of them look at you.'

I wasn't quite sure what he meant by a 'go-faster' surgeon, but I went to see one of them willingly enough. A quick examination confirmed that I had frost-nip in my fingers and toes. The doctor said that my feet would heal up in time, but that I needed some dental work done. When I told him about the nuclear effluent, he said I should certainly have a blood test.

When I got back to Downing, he said, 'I know I'm asking a lot, but will you talk to 'A' Squadron? They're deploying tonight, and I know they'd appreciate it. You could probably give them a load of help.'

Of course I agreed. So I told the story yet again, this time to about forty guys, and at the end they burst into applause, with everyone wanting to shake my hand.

* * *

Back at Al Jouf, I found myself wondering with other guys in the squadron about what could have happened to the rest of our patrol. I think I believed in my heart of hearts that Vince was dead, and Stan the same – or possibly captured. But I couldn't understand why the other five hadn't come out, or why there was no news of them.

People began to assume that the rest of the patrol had died, and I heard that I would probably have to go on a tour of New Zealand, Australia and all round England to talk to the families of the guys we'd lost.

In spite of everything, I felt reasonably well – so when 'B' Squadron began getting ready to drive into Iraq as the security force on a major re-supply for 'A' and 'D', I asked the CO if I could go with them. Luckily he realized that I was a long way from being fit, and said, 'Not a chance.'

Because my teeth were still so slack, I made arrangements to see a dentist. Before my appointment, I was warned that I mustn't under any circumstances tell him where I'd been. When I got into the surgery, the dentist proved a really sensible, nice guy. He asked his assistant to leave the room. 'There's obviously something wrong,' he said.

'Yes,' I replied, 'I've had a bad eight days.'

'I should say so. What do you do for a living?'

'I test Land Rovers.'

'OK. I'm not interested in what you've done. But your mouth's in a serious state. Your gums show signs of malnutrition; they're receding – that's why they're bleeding. I can see the roots of your teeth. There's a chance you'll lose a few. I'll have to take two out, anyway.'

To this day my gums haven't fully recovered; some teeth are still loose. Otherwise, I made a full physical recovery, though it took six weeks for feeling to come back into my fingers and toes.

A blood test taken in a makeshift hospital on an American airbase revealed nothing wrong – but evidently the doctor who did it missed something, because another test, carried out in the UK, showed that I had a blood disorder, caused by drinking dirty water from the Euphrates.

One doctor, talking about weight loss, told me that it was safe to shed one pound – or about half a kilo – a week. When I told him I'd lost 36 lb, or about 16 kg, in a week, he said it was impossible.

'Well it happened,' I told him.

To which he replied, 'That's not good.'

The mental scars took far longer to heal. In the Gulf I began to suffer from a recurrent nightmare. I'm walking through the dark along a road. Ahead of me I see two hooded figures, dressed in black, on top of a mound. I know they're the two men I killed in the nuclear complex, but still I go up to them to ask directions. The night is very dark, and it's as if black rain is falling. As I come close, I see the eyes of the second man, wide with fright, and at the last second a knife-blade flashes as he makes a lunge at me. At that point I wake up, sweating with terror.

When the dream began, I realized that it was caused by feelings of guilt.

I also felt guilty about Vince. There was I, a fully trained mountain guide, and I'd failed to do the obvious thing of tying him to me when we were going down with exposure. Even if I'd just held him by the hand, or kept him in front of me where I could see him, I might have saved him. I knew the reason was that I had been suffering from exposure too – but that couldn't bring him back. On the other hand, he might have slowed us down so much that the cold would have got the better of us all.

Later, when I was back in the UK, I met Vince's

mum, dad, widow and brothers, and told them the full story. It was hard for them to accept that Vince – who they had envisaged as indestructible – had frozen to death in the desert.

On 24 February 1991, the ground war was launched at last. I spent the time glued to CNN television – there was one big set in the corridor between the hangars. When the Coalition began taking prisoners, we couldn't believe the numbers: 20,000, 40,000, 50,000 – we kept a scoreboard.

In five days, unbelievably, it was all over.

The squadron came back from Al Jouf to Victor, getting ready to go home. Moves were being made to bring 'A' and 'D' Squadrons back as well. Then the OC said that as soon as an aircraft to the UK became available, I would be on it.

Just after the ceasefire I was in one of the hangars when somebody rushed in, shouting, 'Hey! We've seen Dinger on the telly!'

Electrified, I ran back with him to see if I could catch a glimpse. There'd been shots of the Iraqis handing over Allied prisoners.

'Are you sure it was him?'

'Yeah, yeah, it was Dinger all right.'

We sat there, waiting for the next news programme. When it came on, someone shouted, 'There he is!'

Sure enough, it was Dinger – and a moment later we saw Stan as well. Both were in Baghdad. They were wearing orange prison overalls, sitting at a table, on their way to being handed over to the Red Crescent (the local equivalent of our Red Cross). It was easy enough to spot Dinger, but Stan was harder to pick out, because he had lost a lot of weight and had become quite gaunt.

Just to see them was exciting. We knew those two were safe – but what about the others?

There were still five men missing from Bravo Two Zero: Bob, Vince, Legs, Mark and Andy.

In addition, we thought a guy from 'A' Squadron called Jack had been killed on another operation. When we heard through the Regiment that the Iraqis had four more prisoners to release, we reckoned that meant one of our guys must have died as well as Jack. Was that Vince?

Details trickled out slowly. The first to reach us, via Dinger, was that Legs had died from hypothermia after trying to cross the Euphrates. Then, to our amazement, we heard that Jack had survived, and was also about to be released. That meant that another member of Bravo Two Zero must have gone down. Rumours flew about, but there was no official information.

Very soon after that, a message came telling us to pack. I would be on the first aircraft going home. When the Hercules landed at Cyprus and we walked into the terminal, someone said, 'Oh – we've just had some of your guys come into the hospital.' Immediately the OC got on the phone, but – quite rightly – security was tight and nobody was being allowed to speak to the released prisoners, so he had some trouble getting through. In the end he managed it, and I spoke to both Dinger and Stan.

Their voices sounded a bit flat, and I could tell they'd been through a lot; they weren't their normal bouncy selves. But Dinger said, 'Look – I owe you a pint for making me keep my jacket. I reckon it saved my life.'

'That's all right,' I said. 'But what happened? How did we split?'

'We heard an aircraft and went to ground. But I can't say much now. We'll see you when we get to the UK.'

Obviously he didn't want to talk on the phone, but I asked, 'Who else is coming back?'

'Andy and Mark.'

That was all he said. It meant that, besides Legs – and, almost certainly, Vince – Bob Consiglio had gone.

I felt very sad about Bob, good, tough little guy that he was – and immediately I wanted to know what had happened to him.

I also had a brief word with Stan. 'Hey,' I told him. 'You made the wrong decision back there.'

'I know,' he agreed. 'I owe you a few pints on that. I should have stayed with you. I *really* should have stayed . . .'

CHAPTER 17
COUNTING THE COST

When we returned to Hereford, the first thing I found was a note in the guardroom telling me to visit the doctor. An appointment was made that very day at the Queen Elizabeth Hospital in Woolwich. I got there at about 5 p.m.

I don't know what people had been expecting, but they'd scrubbed out an isolation ward just for me. I stuck my head round a pair of double doors, and someone shouted, 'Get out! Get out!' as though I was going to contaminate the whole building. When I said I was from Hereford, they told me they'd been expecting someone to turn up in an NBC suit, glowing all over.

The surgeon was fed up that I was so late. But when I explained I'd gone eight days without food, and might have been contaminated in a nuclear refinery, he became a different man, and asked me to report for tests the next day.

The tests lasted all the next morning and into the afternoon. At the end, I went back into the isolation ward, and the doctor came in and said, 'You'd better take a seat.' His face was sombre – as if he had really bad news.

'You've got a viral infection,' he said. 'It will work its way through your body.' He also found that I had a blood disorder, and an abnormal amount of enzymes in my liver produced as a reaction to poisoning. On the nuclear front, I was also tested for radioactive poisoning, but there appeared to be no contamination; he did mention leukaemia, but he brushed aside the possibility. That didn't stop me worrying about it, though . . .

Back in Hereford, we pieced together what had happened to the rest of the patrol. I'd only been home about three days when Stan phoned and came round to my house. He said the worst thing he'd ever done in his life was to ignore my warnings in the wadi.

He told me that he had walked for about four

hours with the goatherd. Towards evening they saw a small group of buildings, with vehicles outside them. Stan approached them on his own. As he arrived, an Arab in a fine-looking white dishdash came out of the building, heading for a Toyota Land Cruiser. Stan tried to engage him in friendly chat, but the man made a dive for the vehicle. Thinking he might have a gun there, Stan fired a single shot through the window and dropped him.

The sound of gunfire brought about eight militiamen, armed with AK-47s, hurtling out of the building, and a firefight broke out. Stan dropped the first, and the second, but then his ammunition ran out, so he leaped into the vehicle. The key was on the floor, under the body of the first Arab. Before he could start the engine the windscreen smashed in on him and a weapon was stuck into his face. Guys dragged him out and were immediately on top of him.

He was captured.

The militiamen bundled him into another car and drove him to the nearest town. At first he was treated well; but later he was kept blindfolded and starved, and was beaten so badly that his skull was fractured. Early in February he had been moved to a base camp near Baghdad; there he was reunited in a cell with Andy and Dinger.

We assumed that after Stan had been captured, the goatherd must have told the militia that there was a second runaway out in the wadi, and directed the party that came in search of me.

Stan and I wondered what would have happened if we'd stayed together, or walked down the railway line. In fact, if there'd been two of us, I think we'd both have been captured. Lonely as it was to be on my own, I was probably better off. There was only one person to hide, one made less noise than two, and there was no chance that the pair of us would talk ourselves into doing something stupid. We probably would have broken into a house in search of food, and that might have led to our capture.

Being alone was what had saved me.

Happily, Stan made a full recovery. He'd had a real battering, but he was able to bounce quickly back to normal.

I also tried to find out what had happened when the patrol split. Andy, who was four back down the column, had heard a jet overhead. He had immediately gone down on one knee in an attempt to contact the pilot on his TACBE, calling out to Vince ahead of him, 'Go to ground!' He had been so busy trying to raise the pilot that he hadn't realized that Vince had never heard his call, and had carried on. We never did work out how we'd become so widely separated, though.

Andy told me that after trying to contact the aircraft, his party saw movement up ahead. They went to ground, and three figures came walking across their front. They assumed this was an Iraqi patrol and let them disappear into the night.

The five picked themselves up and started walking to the north-west, and when dawn came they laid up for the day in the lee of a mound. Because of the snow, rain, wind and bitter cold, Mark started to go down with exposure, so the group decided to risk a daylight move. They made good progress until they reached a main road, where they planned to hijack a vehicle.

Bob leaned on Andy's shoulder and pretended to be wounded. They flagged down a car which turned out to be a taxi. As it stopped, the other three came up out of cover and surrounded it. Kicking out the driver and two other passengers, they took one man with them, because he looked so scared that they thought he might help. They set off westwards along the highway.

All went well until they reached a vehicle control point. Some way short of it they got out of the car, and arranged with their driver that he would drive through the control and pick them up on the other side. In fact, he shopped them, and they had to escape into the desert.

Moving north towards the Euphrates, they found themselves in an area of habitation. By then they reckoned they were only ten kilometres from the river; but behind them military vehicles began to pull up on the highway. Troops poured out and opened fire. The rounds went well over them, but then three or four anti-aircraft guns opened up as well. On the whole this was helpful, as it made locals think an air raid was in progress and run for cover.

The patrol reached the bank of the Euphrates and took a GPS fix. This confirmed that they were only ten kilometres from the border. By then it was dark. They thought about trying to cross the river, but decided that the risk of going down with exposure was too high. In the end they decided to keep heading west, with the hope of reaching the border that night.

They stumbled upon enemy positions, and got into contacts. Creeping, crawling, working their way forward through ploughed fields and along hedges, they made slow progress. Andy, Mark and Bob had a contact during which Bob got split off and ended up in a contact of his own, and Legs and Dinger also got separated.

Bob held the Iraqis off for thirty minutes, single-handed, before he was shot and killed outright. To have defended himself like that for half an hour, against a force of maybe a dozen Iraqis, was quite a feat. At the end, I feel certain, he must have run out of rounds, but not before taking out a lot of Iraqis. I think he was the bravest man in the patrol, because he saved everyone else's lives by holding off the enemy. After the war he was awarded a posthumous Military Medal.

With Bob cut off on his own, Mark got shot in the arm and ankle. He and Andy split up. In the end Andy was captured only a couple of kilometres from the border. He must have been somewhere very close to the line of my own route.

Legs and Dinger, on their own now, went towards

the Euphrates, but soon ran on to another enemy position. Suddenly they heard a weapon cocked, and something shouted in Iraqi, from only ten metres ahead. They let fly a hail of automatic fire from the 203 and Minimi, and received only half a dozen rounds in return. They retreated to the river bank, but by then enemy were closing on them from the east, firing occasional bursts.

They tried to cross the river, but found themselves on a little island, with the main channel still to cross. Only 200 metres upstream, a big road-bridge spanned the whole Euphrates. They could see several vehicles parked on it, and people shining flashlights down onto the water. They heard gunfire in the distance. After waiting an hour, during which they became very cold, they decided their only option was to swim the second channel. Luckily Legs had found a polystyrene box. They broke this into pieces, which they stuffed into the fronts of their smocks to help them float. Then they waded out and swam.

The water was icy, the current strong; they found it hard to make progress, and had to let go their weapons. Legs, who was going down with hypothermia, began to fail. When he fell back,

Dinger got hold of him and towed him on. Reaching the far bank, Dinger dragged him out, but Legs had become incoherent, and couldn't walk.

Daylight revealed a small tin pump house some fifteen metres from the shore. Dinger pulled Legs into it, but he was so far gone that he kept trying to crawl back into the river. Inside the shelter Dinger lit his remaining hexi-block and brewed up a cup of hot water, hoping it would revive his companion. Legs, however, was making no sense, and instead of drinking the hot water, he hit the mug away. When the sun rose, Dinger dragged him out into it, in the hope that it would warm and dry him, but he was too far gone. His skin remained cold, and his eyes flickered meaninglessly back and forth.

When farmers appeared and started to work in the fields, Dinger pulled Legs back into the hut. Then at mid-morning a man with some children in tow came within ten metres of the pump house. Seeing that he was about to be compromised, Dinger showed himself to the farmer, who locked the two soldiers in and ran off shouting. By that time Legs' smock was dry, but he was slipping into unconsciousness. Clearly he could not move, so Dinger burst his way through the roof of the hut and made off towards the north, away from the river.

His plan was to pull the enemy away from Legs and give him a chance to recover.

Dinger was spotted almost immediately and followed by a posse of locals, who soon swelled into a crowd. He tried to do a runner, but was caught by the mob, one of whom wanted to cut off one of his ears. The guy was actually holding his ear when Dinger managed to bring out one of his sovereigns. The people fought over that, but then realized he had more, and he started handing them out, which cooled them down.

They walked him into a village, where the people went wild and beat him to the ground before he was handed over to the police. While in the police station, Dinger saw Legs being brought in on a stretcher. He was quickly loaded into an ambulance and driven away, but although Dinger watched closely, he saw no movement, and feared that his companion was already dead.

And that was the end of a brave escape attempt.

By the next night, when I had my own contact and made the Euphrates, the survivors were in jail, being questioned by the Iraqis. They were all brutally beaten for several days, partly in the course of interrogation, partly by their guards, who hit them casually whenever they saw a chance. Even Mark was beaten on his wounded ankle. I was glad that I had been tortured by weather, thirst and hunger rather than by human beings.

In Hereford, together with the Int Officer and a decent map, I worked out the exact distances I had walked.

On the first night, before and after the split, we covered 70 km.

On the second night Stan and I made 40 km, losing Vince in the middle.

On the third I walked another 40 km to reach the Euphrates.

The fourth night was the most frustrating, as I had to cover 40 km in zigzags and boxes to make only 10 km towards the border.

On the fifth night I advanced 30 km and then did another 5 to 6 km during the day, up into the wadis.

The sixth night took me into and out of the nuclear refinery – another 30 km.

The last and most terrible night I did between 40 and 50 km – most of them unnecessarily.

The total came to nearly 300 kilometres, or about 186 miles!

I found that people were beginning to compare my escape with that of SAS legend Jack Sillito, who trekked for more than 100 miles through the Western Desert of North Africa in 1942, having been stranded behind German lines. Without realizing it, I had easily beaten Sillito's distance. But in fact, the two escapes were made in widely different circumstances. Whereas my main enemy was cold, his had been heat, and he had no river to give him water or guide him. Instead, he had navigated by the sun and the stars, and scrounged liquid from condensation in abandoned jerry cans.

At the end of June I heard the good news that in the Gulf War honours list I had been awarded the Military Medal. It was all very splendid going to London, and an honour to meet the Queen, but I would have much preferred to have received the Military Medal in front of the whole Regiment. I knew that the medal-winners included some of the bravest soldiers in the world, and every one had been fully earned.

* * *

Even now, many years later, I still see incidents from the patrol, and hear the sounds, as clear as day.

I see rounds flying between us during the first contact.

I see Stan walking off down the wadi with the goatherd.

I see the two hooded Arabs waiting for me on top of the mound.

I try to put the images from my mind, but they creep back in.

More and more I realize how lucky I was not to be shot, not to be captured, not to be caught up in the barbed wire on the border. Sometimes I feel that I must have used up all my luck.

All in all, my experience taught me a good deal about myself. Most people, I think, don't know what they're capable of until they're put to the test. Before the Gulf War, if somebody had told me I could walk nearly 300 kilometres through enemy territory in seven nights, with no food and practically no water, with inadequate clothes, no proper sleep and no shelter, I wouldn't have believed them.

When I had to, I did it. Whether I could do it a second time is another matter.

Back then I was at a peak of physical fitness, and armed with the skills, the endurance, the competitive instinct and the motivation which SAS training had given me. But I really hope I'll never have to do something like that again.

Once in a lifetime is enough.

AUTHOR'S HISTORICAL NOTE

Although Saddam Hussein was forced to withdraw from Kuwait, he remained in power as the President of Iraq. The regime was widely perceived to be oppressive, including atrocities against specific members of the Iraqi community, and ultimately UK forces were involved in a second war against Iraq which began in 2003.

The invasion of Iraq led to an occupation and the eventual capture of Saddam Hussein, who was later tried in an Iraqi court of law and executed by the new Iraqi government.

The situation in Iraq remains unstable.

Read on for a preview of
Chris Ryan's brand-new series

AGENT 21

'I work for a government agency. You don't need
to know which one . . . The people we are looking
for are of a very particular type . . . You fit a profile,
Zak,' the old man said. 'A very precise one.'

Zak Darke becomes Agent 21.

What happened to the twenty agents before him he
doesn't know yet.

What he does know is that his life is about to change
for ever . . .

PROLOGUE

It didn't take them long to die. It never does. Not if you do it right.

Al and Janet Darke had been looking forward to their trip. Lagos in Nigeria might not have been their first choice, but as the university where they worked had paid for them to come here for an international climate-change conference, they didn't want to miss the opportunity of travelling around a bit once it was over.

They were a quiet couple. They kept themselves to themselves. They had both felt a bit scared when their taxi drove them from the airport into the busy, noisy, dirty city of Lagos. Cars sat in traffic jams, bumper to bumper. Their fumes made it difficult to breathe. Some of the buildings they passed looked quite grand; others were just shacks made out of metal sheets. And there were thousands upon thousands of people, everywhere. It made Oxford Street at Christmas look like a desert island.

So when they arrived at their hotel – a posh one called the InterContinental, bang in the middle of the city – they holed up in their room for a bit. Getting used to the heat and to being in a strange place. A shower. Some food.

'Zak would like it here,' Janet said as they stood on their balcony and looked out over the chaos.

'If Zak was here,' Al replied, 'he'd be out there nosing around already. You know what he's like.'

Janet smiled. Yeah, she knew.

It felt weird coming away without their son, but it was 22 April and the summer term had just started so they didn't have much choice. Not that a couple of weeks out of school would have harmed him. Zak was a smart kid. Good with his hands. Good with his brain. The kind of boy who knew how to take care of himself. He had seemed perfectly happy to be staying with Janet's sister and her family. Vivian and Godfrey were a bit severe, but Zak got on well with his cousin Ellie. His parents were sure they'd be having a good time.

The sun set about 7 p.m. – a blood-red ball that drenched Lagos with its glow before it plunged into darkness. Al and Janet dressed for dinner and prepared to meet the other conference delegates who'd come from all over the world. They wouldn't know anyone – not even any of the eleven other British guests – and they were glad to have each other.

The dining hall was splendidly set. To look at it, you wouldn't know that barely a mile from this hotel there existed one of the seediest slums in the world, so poor that the people who lived there had to use the streets as a toilet. Here were crisp, white tablecloths, fizzy water in bottles and appetizing baskets of freshly baked bread rolls. There were five large round tables, each with ten place settings, and a table plan pinned to a board by the entrance. When Janet and Al checked it they saw, to their relief, that they were sitting next to each other. To Janet's right there was a professor from Helsinki in Finland; to Al's left an American journalist. The couple accepted a glass of wine from a smartly dressed waiter with a tray of drinks, then went to find their seats.

The Finnish professor was an eccentric-looking man with a bald head but a bushy white beard. He was already sitting down when they approached, but stood up when he saw Janet. 'Allow me,' he said, and he pulled out her seat for her. 'My name is Jenssen. It is very nice to meet you . . .' He glanced at the name tag on Janet's place setting. 'Dr Darke.'

Janet smiled. 'And you, Professor Jenssen.'

The American journalist didn't arrive until everyone else was sitting and the waiters were serving the starter. He was hugely fat, and had sweat pouring down his face. 'Africa,' he said with a huff as he plonked himself down on his seat. 'Every time I come here, I promise myself I'll never come back. Perhaps I should listen to myself a bit more.'

Perhaps you should, thought Al Darke, but he didn't say it out loud. Instead, he thanked the waiter who had just placed a plate of food in front of him. Slices of colourful fruit were laid out on the plate like a fan, with some kind of dressing drizzled over the top.

'This looks delicious,' Al said.

'Give it three days,' the journalist replied. 'You'll be begging for a cheeseburger.' Al saw, though, that he tucked in to his food with gusto.

Al was halfway through his starter when he noticed that his nose was running. Embarrassed, he grabbed his napkin and held it to his face. By the time he had covered his face, though, he felt moisture seeping from his eyes and his vision was blurred. He turned to look at Janet. Her eyes were wet too, the pupils as small as pinpricks.

'What's happening?' Al started to say. But as he spoke, his chest collapsed into a fit of coughing and he found himself struggling for breath.

'*Al . . .*' Janet was looking at him with fear on her face.

The pain came next – a horrible, sharp needling behind the eyes and in the throat. Al felt dizzy. He looked around the room. About half of the guests had stood up, and from the way they clutched their heads and throats, it was clear they were suffering the same symptoms. At the far end of the room, one man collapsed. Al was half aware of the waiters, buzzing around them like panicked bees. They didn't know what was happening any more than the diners.

Al felt himself slump in his seat. He couldn't help it – it was as though his muscles had turned to jelly and he had lost the power to control them, even in order to breathe. His eyes fell on the half-eaten fruit. The bright colours of the mango and papaya looked ten times brighter, and they burned into his retinas. He turned to his wife.

'The food,' he said.

Janet Darke didn't hear him. For her the room was spinning more violently. People were shouting around her, but all she could really concentrate on was the nausea. She wanted to be sick, but was too weak to do even that.

Al and Janet weren't the first to die. The professor from Helsinki was already slumped on the table, his face in his half-eaten plate of fruit; and the American journalist was twitching on the ground. They knew it was coming, though. With what little strength they had left, they reached out with their hands and clasped their fingers together.

When the Nigerian police arrived half an hour later, they needed to prize Al and Janet Darke's hands away from each other before they could remove the bodies.

PART ONE

CHAPTER 1
THE SHADOW

Six months later

'Darke!'

Giggling in the classroom.

'*Darke!*'

Zak looked up. He'd been staring out of the window, where the late afternoon sun was glowing over the school football pitch. He had a pencil in his hand, which he twirled through his fingers. On his table there was a circuit board. It was covered with transistors and diodes and connected to a small loudspeaker.

'Zachary Darke,' his physics teacher, Mr Peters, said in a nasal voice. Peters had bad skin, square glasses and a tragic dress sense. He'd only been teaching at the Camden High School in North London for six weeks, but in that time he'd managed to make himself unpopular with pretty much everyone. 'You've got ten minutes left to complete your assignment. I don't think staring out of the window is a very good way to—'

He was interrupted by a noise. Zak had flicked a switch and the sound of Lady Gaga singing 'Just Dance' filled the room. The physics teacher *had* told them to construct a transistor radio, after all.

Peters was a total nightmare. He loved to set his classes almost impossible tasks and watch them squirm as they failed to complete them. All of them except Zak. He was good at stuff like this, but even that didn't seem to impress Peters. The jokers at the back singing along to the music didn't impress him either. His pockmarked neck turned red. 'Turn it off, boy.'

'Yes, sir,' Zak replied. He stared back out of the window.

Mr Peters walked up to Zak's table. Zak had grown tall in the last year – taller than a few of the teachers, even. It meant that some of them, like Peters, puffed themselves up when talking to him. 'Showing off isn't a very attractive habit, Darke,' he said.

'I wasn't, sir. I was just—'

'Quiet. I don't want to hear another word from you.'

'No, sir,' Zak said, and went back to his daydreaming.

He had plenty to daydream about.

When the police had showed up six months ago on the doorstep of his uncle and aunt's house to tell him what had happened, they had said it was food poisoning. An acute case, a terrible accident. It had affected everyone in the hotel dining hall that night. Fifty of them. And for a while Zak had believed them. Why wouldn't he? The story had made it onto the news, and he was too shocked and upset anyway to think about it much.

But as time passed and the Nigerian police had refused to release his parents' bodies for burial, Zak had grown suspicious. If it had been just food poisoning, then why the delay? Why couldn't they just send his mum and dad back so they could have a proper funeral? And what was so virulent that it could kill fifty people at a single sitting? Zak had hit the Internet, done his research. There was botulism; *e. coli*, maybe. But Mum and Dad had been in good health. Those kind of bacteria might have made them feel very unwell, but kill them? And everyone else they were dining with? Not likely.

When school finished, he walked home with his cousin Ellie. She was in the year above, but they were good friends. This walking-home-together thing was a new one, though. Zak used to skateboard everywhere on the board his mum and dad had got him for his thirteenth birthday. However, he didn't have the heart to use it now, which was why he preferred to walk.

Ellie chattered away like she always did. Zak's cousin was a tall, pretty girl with long, honey-coloured hair and one of those friendly, open faces that people quickly take a shine to. Zak heard her, but didn't listen. Something else had caught his attention.

For two weeks now, maybe three, Zak had had the strangest feeling. More than once, he'd thought he was going mad. He knew that nobody could *really* be following him, but it happened almost every day – twice a day, sometimes – that he was walking down the street, or buying something in a shop, or doing whatever he was doing, and he'd get that familiar, unpleasant feeling. A hotness on the back of his neck. A tingling.

At first, he would turn and look around. But he never saw anybody. Or he saw lots of people, just walking past or milling about. After a bit, he didn't bother to turn. Instead, he would keep walking and try to look out of the corner of his eye. That was more successful. He'd sometimes be able to sense somebody walking along the opposite side of the road, or standing by the school gates. Whenever he turned to look, however, the person was gone. It was like they had a sixth sense – although Zak's sensible side told him that was impossible . . .

He had the feeling now. They were walking along Camden Road. It was busy with the early rush-hour traffic, and the pavements were full of school kids. But there was something else – like a dark shadow on the edge of his vision, walking in the same direction on the opposite pavement.

Zak looked firmly ahead and tuned his ears in to Ellie's conversation.

'. . . so *I* told her that there was no way I was going if—'

'Ellie, shh.'

She looked at him. 'Don't be so rude,' she said.

'Sorry. But listen, you see that turning up ahead to the right?'

Ellie looked ahead to see what he meant. It was a small turning about fifteen metres away that led into a little cobbled mews road. 'Jasmine Mews?'

'When we get there, turn into it, then run like hell to the end and hide.'

'Why?' Ellie asked. 'What's going on, Zak?'

'It's just a game,' Zak said. 'I want to play a trick on someone. You up for it?'

Ellie shrugged. 'Suppose so,' she said.

They continued to walk. Just as they reached the side street, Zak and Ellie turned sharply; and the moment they were out of sight of the main road, they ran down the cobbled mews.

There were only a few cars parked here, outside the small, cottage-like houses. At the end of the street was an alley running at right angles. They turned left into it, then stopped, out of breath. Zak pressed his back against the wall and peered round the corner.

He saw a man. From a distance it was difficult to make out his features, but he was quite tall, maybe in his sixties with a tanned face and scruffy, shoulder-length hair. The man stood at the end of the mews for just long enough to see that it was deserted. Then he quickly turned and walked away.

Zak felt Ellie tapping his shoulder. 'What's going on?' she whispered.

'I don't know,' said Zak, his voice a million miles away. 'I just don't know.'

The next day was Saturday. Zak woke early. He always did these days. Since his parents' death, sleep was hard to come by. He got dressed and went downstairs.

To his surprise, his aunt was already up. She was standing in the small kitchen, her hair in a net and a cigarette in her hand, boiling the kettle. She looked over her shoulder, saw Zak then turned her attention back to her tea-making. No 'good morning'. No nothing. He shrugged and headed back towards the stairs.

His uncle and aunt – Vivian and Godfrey Lewis – didn't want him there, and they weren't afraid to show it. After Mum and Dad had died in Nigeria, they'd agreed to take him in. It had been a choice between them or moving up to Macclesfield where his other cousin, Ben, lived. But Zak hadn't really wanted to relocate north, and Ben had a habit of ending up in crazy situations. So Vivian and Godfrey it was, and they didn't let a day go by without reminding Zak in some small way that he wasn't really welcome in the small terraced house of 63 Acacia Drive.

'Zak!'

His aunt was at the bottom of the stairs. He turned round to look at her.

'We're taking Ellie out for the day. Lunch and then a movie. You'll be all right here, won't you?'

Zak tried not to look disappointed. 'Yeah,' he replied. 'I'll be fine, Aunt Vivian.'

He continued walking up the stairs.

Ellie was in the doorway of her bedroom, still in her pyjamas. She had obviously heard her mum, and as Zak walked past, she mouthed the words 'I'm sorry' at him. He gave her a smile – it wasn't her fault, after all – then continued towards his room.

A tap on his shoulder. Ellie had followed him and as he turned round she gave him a hug. 'I wish you could come with us,' she said.

Zak smiled. There was something about Ellie that always made him feel better. 'I'll be fine,' he said. 'Have a nice day, yeah?'

Ellie and her parents left at half past nine. The house was quiet. Zak spent some time on the family computer – he'd installed some plug-ins that kept his browsing history private, just in case he got in trouble for using it. But it was sunny outside and he felt cooped up. He decided to go for a walk.

There was a garage at the end of the road. Zak stopped off there and bought himself a can of Coke with the last of his change. He'd inherited what little money his mum and dad had, but it was in trust and his uncle and aunt weren't exactly the generous types – at least, not when it came to Zak.

He walked to the park. It was busy – lots of younger kids out playing football or mucking about on the swings. A few people walking their dogs. Zak sat apart from them all on a wooden bench in the dappled shade of a tree. He sipped his Coke slowly and watched everybody enjoying their Saturday morning.

By the time Zak saw him, he didn't know how long the man had been standing there. He was about fifty metres away, alone by the park railings and looking directly at Zak. He had hair down to his shoulders and a tanned, lined face. There was no doubt about it – he was the same man who had followed him and Ellie yesterday.

Zak felt himself crushing the Coke can slightly. Half of him wanted to stand up and rush away; the other half wanted to sit here. To stare the guy out.

The other half won.

Zak felt his skin prickling as the man walked towards him. Even though it was hot, the man wore a heavy coat and had his hands plunged into the pockets. He didn't look directly at Zak, but kept his gaze elsewhere; and when he sat next to him on the bench, he barely seemed to know that Zak was there. He removed a silver cigarette case from his pocket and lit a thin, black cigarillo. The sickly smell of cherry tobacco filled the air.

Zak played it cool. He took a sip from his Coke before speaking. 'Feel like telling me why you've been playing follow-my-leader?' he asked.

'It's a beautiful day, Zak. A lovely day for a walk.'

Zak tried not to look surprised that the man knew his name.

'Tell me what you want, or I'm out of here.'

Only now did the man look at him. He had piercing green eyes that looked rather youthful despite his leathery tanned face and long, grey hair. He also looked mildly surprised. 'You're free to go, of course, Zak, at any time at all.'

A pause.

'So why have you?' Zak asked.

'Why have I what, Zak?'

'Been following me?'

The man smiled. 'Because I'm interested in you, Zak. I was very sorry, by the way, to hear about your parents.'

'You seem to know a lot about me,' Zak said.

'Oh,' the man replied, 'I do. More than you might imagine. Congratulations, incidentally, on your achievement in your physics lesson yesterday. I understand that you were the only one who succeeded in making a transistor radio. A sound knowledge of electronics could be a useful skill, in certain lines of work.'

As he said this, he raised an eyebrow. It made Zak feel distinctly uncomfortable. He downed the rest of his Coke, crushed the can completely and stood up. 'I'm out of here,' he said. 'Stop following me, all right, otherwise I'll call the police, tell them I've got my very own stalker.'

The old man inclined his head, as if to say, *It's your choice*. Zak started walking away.

'Just one thing, Zak.' The man's voice stopped him short, but he didn't turn round. 'If you want to know the real reason your mum and dad died, we might want to talk some more.'

Zak didn't look back. He didn't say anything. But he didn't move either.

'I'll be here tomorrow,' the man continued. 'Half past eleven. Think about it.'

Elsewhere in the park, children were shrieking with pleasure. A cloud briefly covered the sun, then drifted away again. Zak experienced it all in slow motion as the old man's words echoed in his head.

He turned.

The wooden bench was empty. And when he cast around trying to find where the stranger had gone, the old man was nowhere to be seen.

HAVE YOU TRIED CHRIS RYAN'S ACTION-PACKED FICTION?

*You wake up alone in a dark room.
You are gagged and forced into a
waiting truck
What would you do?*

AND DON'T MISS THE **ALPHA FORCE** SERIES!